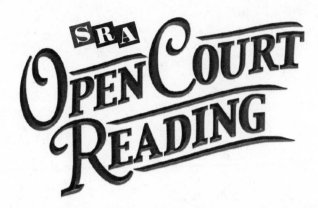

SRA OPEN COURT READING

Decodable Takehome Books

Level 1
Practice Books 49-97

A Division of The McGraw·Hill Companies

Columbus, Ohio

www.sra4kids.com

SRA/McGraw-Hill

A Division of The McGraw·Hill Companies

Send all inquiries to:
SRA/McGraw-Hill
8787 Orion Place
Columbus, OH 43240-4027

ISBN 0-07-572312-3

 2 3 4 5 6 7 8 9 QPD 06 05 04 03 02

Contents

About the Takehome Books

The *SRA Open Court Reading Decodable Books* allow your students to apply their knowledge of phonic elements to read simple, engaging texts. Each story supports instruction in a new phonic element and incorporates elements and words that have been learned earlier.

The students can fold and staple the pages of each *Decodable Takehome Book* to make books of their own to keep and read. We suggest that you keep extra sets of the stories in your classroom for the children to reread.

How to make a Takehome Book

1. Tear out the pages you need.

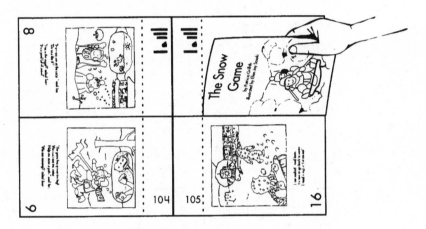

2. Place pages 4 and 5, and pages 2 and 7 faceup.

3. Place pages 4 and 5 on top of pages 2 and 7.

4. Fold along the center line.

5. Check to make sure the pages are in order.

6. Staple the pages along the fold.

Just to let you know...

A message from _____

Help your child discover the joy of independent reading with *SRA Open Court Reading*. From time to time your child will bring home his or her very own *Decodable Takehome Books* to share with you. With your help, these stories can give your child important reading practice and a joyful shared reading experience.

You may want to set aside a few minutes every evening to read these stories together. Here are some suggestions you may find helpful:

- Do not expect your child to read each story perfectly, but concentrate on sharing the book together.
- Participate by doing some of the reading.
- Talk about the stories as you read, give lots of encouragement, and watch as your child becomes more fluent throughout the year!

Learning to read takes lots of practice. Sharing these stories is one way that your child can gain that valuable practice. Encourage your child to keep the *Decodable Takehome Books* in a special place. This collection will make a library of books that your child can read and reread. Take the time to listen to your child read from his or her library. Just a few moments of shared reading each day can give your child the confidence needed to excel in reading.

Children who read every day come to think of reading as a pleasant, natural part of life. One way to inspire your child to read is to show that reading is an important part of your life by letting him or her see you reading books, magazines, newspapers, or any other materials. Another good way to show that you value reading is to share a *Decodable Takehome Book* with your child each day.

Successful reading experiences allow children to be proud of their new-found reading ability. Support your child with interest and enthusiasm about reading. You won't regret it!

SRA Open Court Reading

Just Ten Cents

by Amy D. Charles Peter
illustrated by Barry Mullins

Practice Book 49

A Division of The McGraw-Hill Companies

Columbus, Ohio

9

I am Alice.

8

www.sra4kids.com

SRA/McGraw-Hill

A Division of The McGraw-Hill Companies

Copyright © 2002 by SRA/McGraw-Hill.

All rights reserved. Except as permitted under the United States Copyright Act, no part of this publication may be reproduced or distributed in any form or by any means, or stored in a database or retrieval system, without prior written permission from the publisher.

Printed in the United States of America.

Send all inquiries to:
SRA/McGraw-Hill
8787 Orion Place
Columbus, OH 43240-4027

2

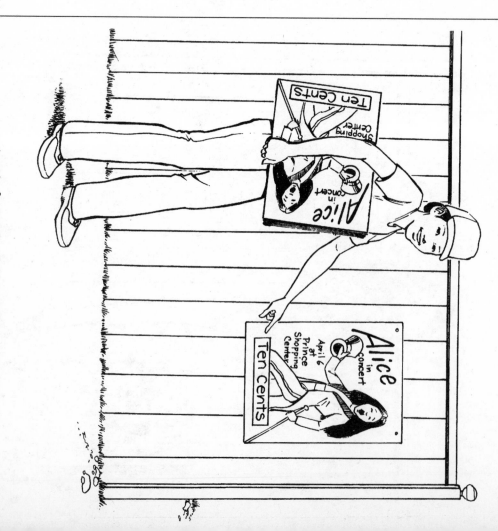

A ticket is just ten cents.
But not for me.

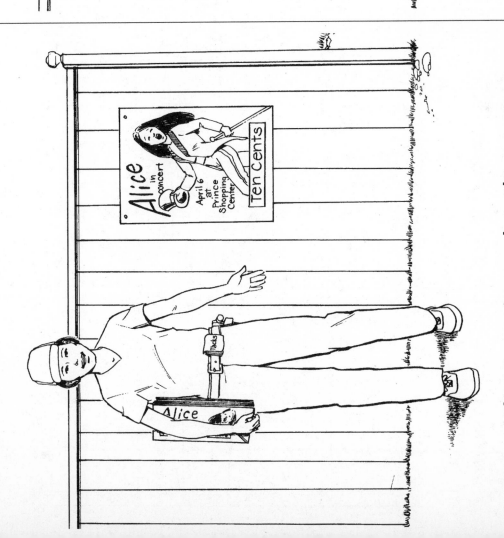

I tacked that ad on the fence.
It tells of a concert.

3

Since Alice practices a lot, the concert
will be a big hit.

6

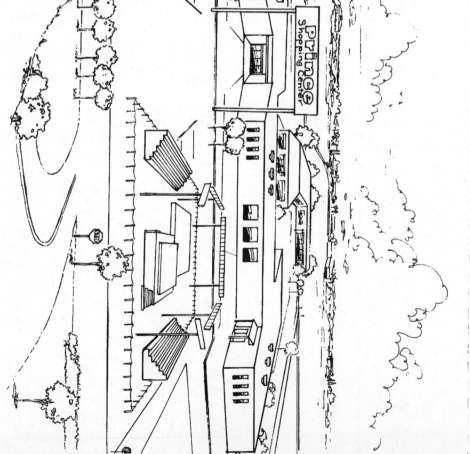

The concert is at the shopping center.

4

The concert has a band and dancers.
The star is Alice.
Alice is the singer.

5

Open Court Reading

Cilla's Fun

by Clare Daniel
illustrated by Kersti Frigell

Practice Book 50

SRA

A Division of The McGraw-Hill Companies

Columbus, Ohio

Cilla is with Francis at a skating rink.
Cinderella is on skates.
Cinderella is dancing with a prince!
Cilla thinks this is the best place!

www.sra4kids.com

SRA/McGraw-Hill

A Division of The McGraw-Hill Companies

Copyright © 2002 by SRA/McGraw-Hill.

Send all inquiries to:
SRA/McGraw-Hill
8787 Orion Place
Columbus, OH 43240-4027

Cilla is with her sister, Grace.
Cilla and Grace are at the cinema.
Cilla wants to see *Cinderella*.
Cinderella has just started at the cinema.
Grace thinks this place is the best!

Cilla is at an art shop with her dad.

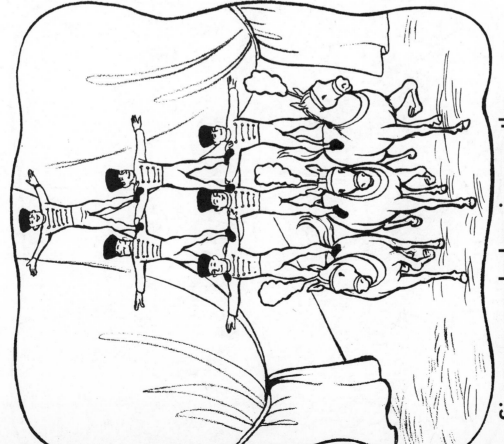

Six men are balancing on the prancing horses.
Mom thinks this place is the best!

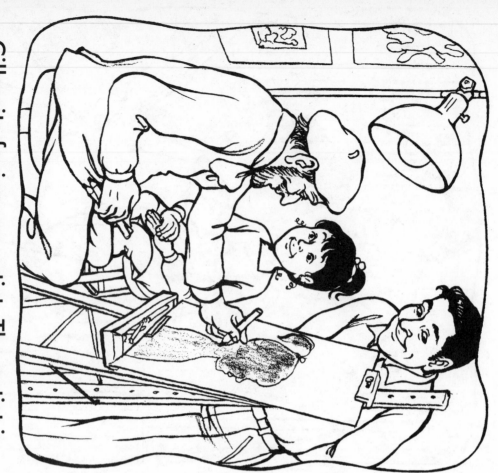

Cilla sits facing an artist. The artist is tracing her face.
Dad thinks this place is the best!

4

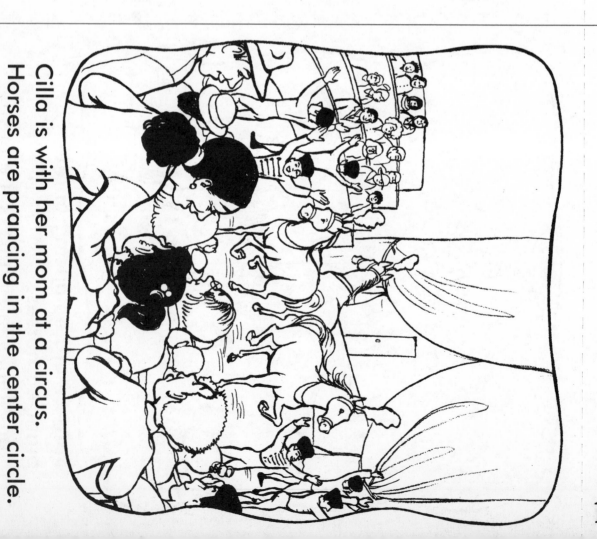

Cilla is with her mom at a circus.
Horses are prancing in the center circle.

5

SRA Open Court Reading

Brian's Spiders

by Cindy Wilkinson
illustrated by Shawn McManus

Practice Book 51

SRA

A Division of *The McGraw-Hill Companies*

Columbus, Ohio

17

Some children and adults are
scared of spiders, but not me.
I make spiders to hang on my wall.

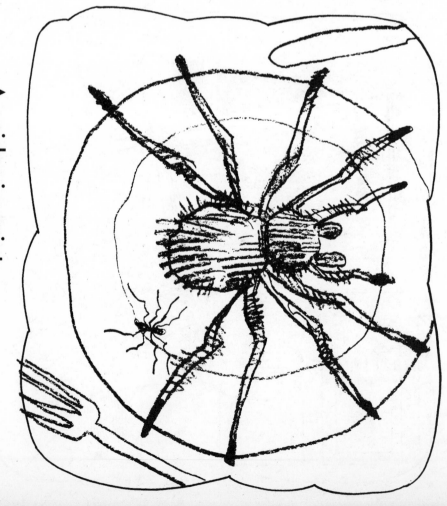

A spider is quiet.
A spider can be big.
A spider can be small.
A spider can look like an ant.

Hi, I'm Brian.
I'm going to tell you of
the spiders I make.

3

Spiders munch on bugs.
Spiders munch on fish.
Big spiders can munch on birds!

6

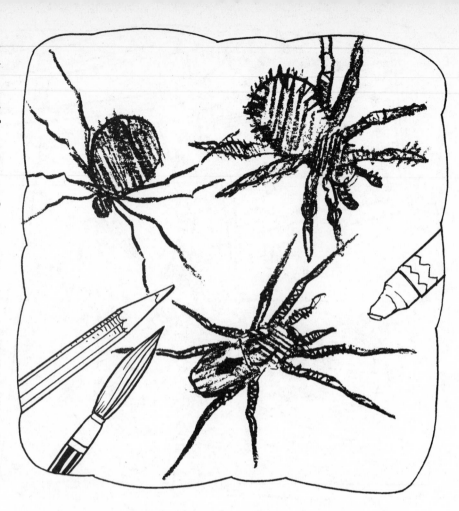

A spider is a bug, but a spider is not an insect.
There are 30,000 kinds of spiders.
All spiders have lots of legs.

4

Spiders can dwell in the grass.
Spiders can dwell in the sand.
Spiders can dwell in the water.

5

SRA Open Court Reading

Brice Likes Limes

by Mitch Olson
illustrated by Kersti Frigell

Practice Book 52

SRA

A Division of The McGraw-Hill Companies

Columbus, Ohio

Brice takes a bite.
A lemon is more bitter than a lime!
This time Brice will dine without lemons or limes!

8

Instead Brice finds a nice ripe lemon.
Brice thinks, "Lemons are like limes."

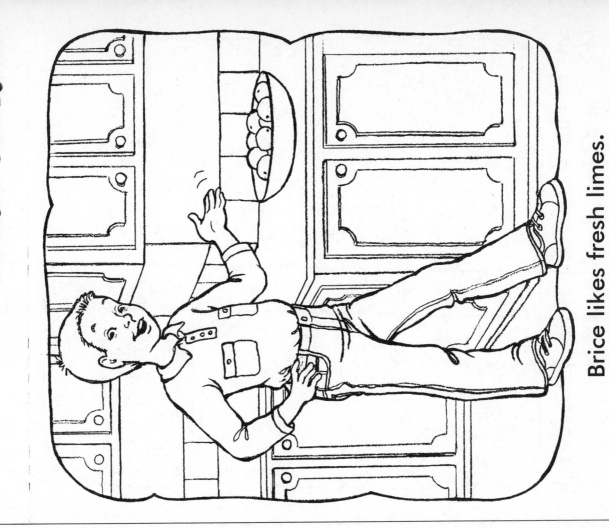

Brice likes fresh limes.

Brice gets inside the pine cabinets but does not find a single lime.

6

Lots of times, Brice squirts limes on his fish when he dines.

4

But now Brice is out of limes!

5

SRA Open Court Reading

Old Gold

by Nathaniel Alexander
illustrated by Kersti Frigell

Practice Book 53

SRA

A Division of The McGraw-Hill Companies

Columbus, Ohio

"But, Mom, Oma got a map from an old chest. It has a mark for old gold."

8

www.sra4kids.com

SRA/McGraw-Hill

A Division of The McGraw-Hill Companies

Copyright © 2002 by SRA/McGraw-Hill.

All rights reserved. Except as permitted under the United States Copyright Act, no part of this publication may be reproduced or distributed in any form or by any means, or stored in a database or retrieval system, without prior written permission from the publisher.

Printed in the United States of America.

Send all inquiries to:
SRA/McGraw-Hill
8787 Orion Place
Columbus, OH 43240-4027

2

"The gold is over here by the fence.
Don't be scared, Tim. Be bold!"

7

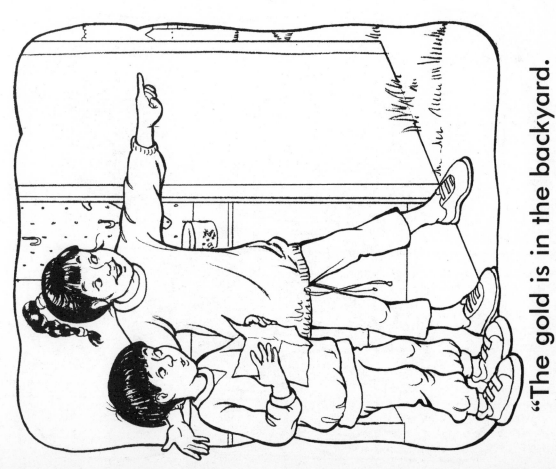

"See this map? I saw it in an old chest."

3

"The gold is in the backyard.
The map told me so."

6

4

"You can hold it.
Go ahead and unfold it."

"The map tells us
where to find old gold."

5

29

SRA Open Court Reading

Simone Awoke!

by Keith Randall
illustrated by Pat Lucas-Morris

Practice Book 54

SRA

A Division of The McGraw-Hill Companies
Columbus, Ohio

Then the alarm awoke Simone!

8

www.sra4kids.com

SRA/McGraw-Hill

A Division of The McGraw-Hill Companies

Copyright © 2002 by SRA/McGraw-Hill.

All rights reserved. Except as permitted under the United States Copyright Act, no part of this publication may be reproduced or distributed in any form or by any means, or stored in a database or retrieval system, without prior written permission from the publisher.

Printed in the United States of America.

Send all inquiries to:
SRA/McGraw-Hill
8787 Orion Place
Columbus, OH 43240-4027

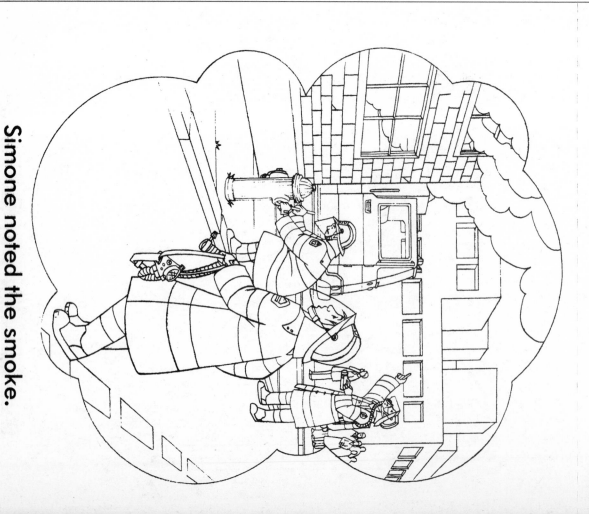

Simone noted the smoke.

The alarm awoke Simone.

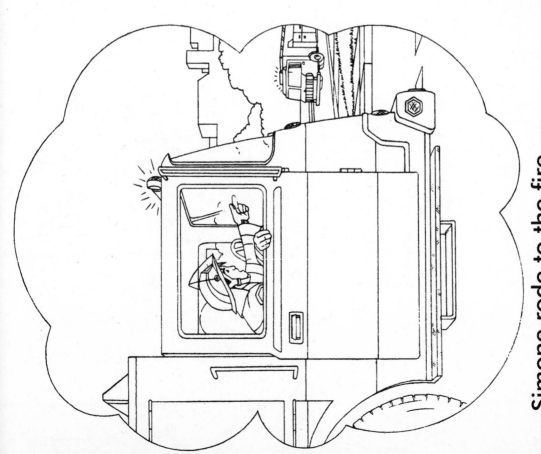

Simone rode to the fire.
She hoped she was not too late.

Simone slid down the pole.

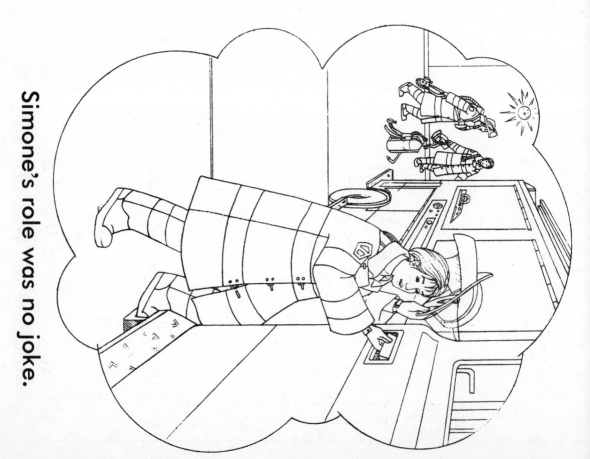

Simone's role was no joke.

SRA OPEN COURT READING

Bev Travels

by Bob Harvey
illustrated by Kersti Frigell

Practice Book 55

SRA
A Division of The McGraw-Hill Companies
Columbus, Ohio

33

Bev quivers! Bev's travel plans have just unraveled!

www.sra4kids.com

SRA/McGraw-Hill

A Division of The McGraw-Hill Companies

Copyright © 2002 by SRA/McGraw-Hill.

Printed in the United States of America.

Send all inquiries to:
SRA/McGraw-Hill
8787 Orion Place
Columbus, OH 43240-4027

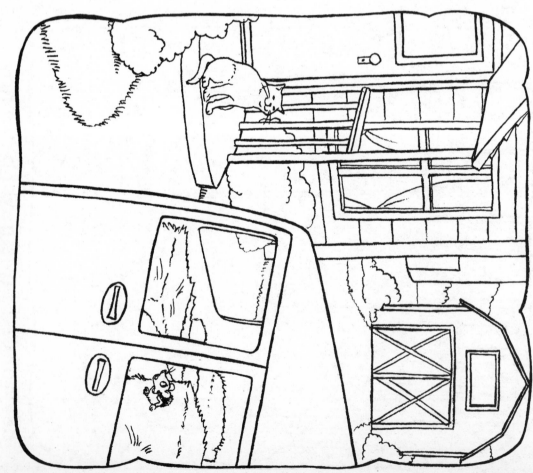

Vic is Evan's cat.

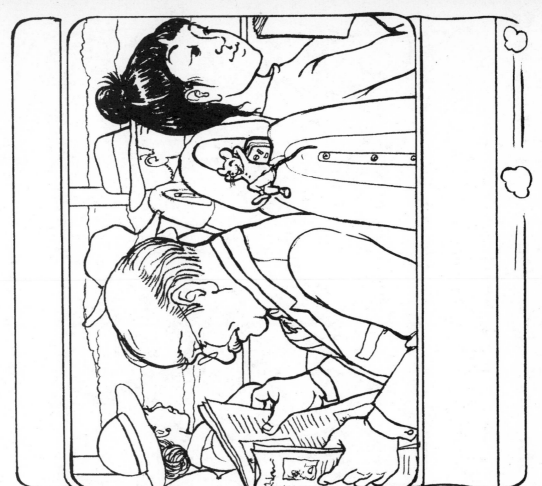

This is Bev. Bev likes to travel.

3

The van is Evan's van.

6

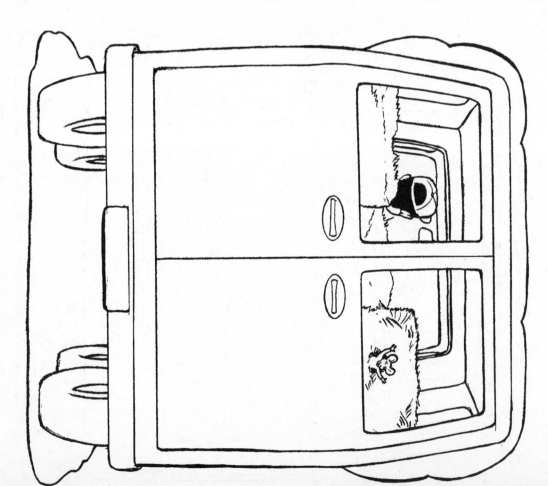

Bev's pals marvel at her tales.

Bev does not drive, but she goes all over.

4

This time Bev hides in a van.

5

SRA Open Court Reading

Hubert's Bugle

by Sharon Frank
illustrated by Len Epstein

Practice Book 56

SRA

A Division of The McGraw-Hill Companies

Columbus, Ohio

Honk

Hubert's bugle helped him have fun!

8

www.sra4kids.com

SRA/McGraw-Hill

A Division of The McGraw-Hill Companies

Copyright © 2002 by SRA/McGraw-Hill.

Send all inquiries to:
SRA/McGraw-Hill
8787 Orion Place
Columbus, OH 43240-4027

Hubert stopped to think. "Perhaps my bugle can help me have fun."

Hubert liked bugle music.

3

But Hubert still could not play the bugle.

6

But Hubert could not play bugle music.

4

Hubert started as a pupil in a bugle music class.

5

41

Pam Is Not Amused

SRA Open Court Reading

by Skip Rodgers
illustrated by Meryl Henderson

Practice Book 57

A Division of The McGraw-Hill Companies

Columbus, Ohio

Pam is excused.
Dad is not amused.

2

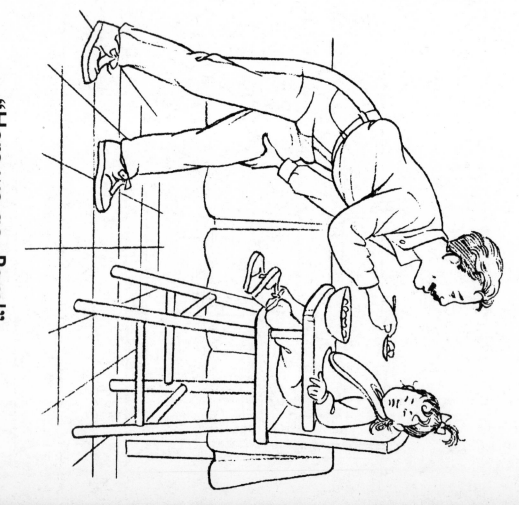

"Here we go, Pam!"
But Pam . . . is not amused.

7

"Excuse me, miss. Let me in."
Pam is not amused.

3

"Is that perfume I smell on Pam?"
Is Pam amused?

6

43

"Excuse me, miss. I'm confused."
Pam is not amused.

"Pam is so cute!"
Pam still is not amused.

SRA Open Court Reading

Marge's Barge

by M. P. Fisher
illustrated by Jan Pyk

Practice Book 58

SRA
A Division of The McGraw-Hill Companies
Columbus, Ohio

Gage felt "Gem" was a good name.
Now Marge's barge is called Gem.

8

www.sra4kids.com

SRA/McGraw-Hill

A Division of The McGraw-Hill Companies

Copyright © 2002 by SRA/McGraw-Hill.

All rights reserved. Except as permitted under the United States Copyright Act, no part of this publication may be reproduced or distributed in any form or by any means, or stored in a database or retrieval system, without prior written permission from the publisher.

Printed in the United States of America.

Send all inquiries to:
SRA/McGraw-Hill
8787 Orion Place
Columbus, OH 43240-4027

"I think General Danger is a strange name," said Gage.

"What can I name it?" asked Marge.

Marge lived on the water.
Marge was in charge of a barge.

3

Marge had a pal. His name was Gage.
Gage suggested Marge change the
name of the barge.

6

4

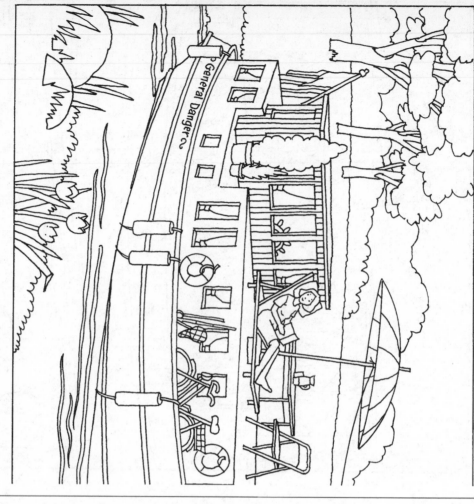

Marge's barge was large.
Marge called her barge
"General Danger."

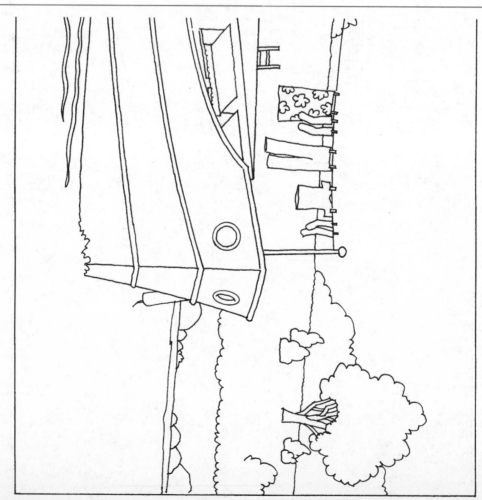

The water rocked the barge.
The rocking was gentle.

5

SRA Open Court Reading

SRA Open Court Reading

Gingerbread Magic

by Maurice P. Fry
illustrated by Shawn McManus

Practice Book 59

SRA
A Division of The McGraw-Hill Companies
Columbus, Ohio

"I must have dozed.
I am glad the gingerbread man
is back on the original pages."

www.sra4kids.com

SRA/McGraw-Hill

A Division of The McGraw-Hill Companies

Copyright © 2002 by SRA/McGraw-Hill.

All rights reserved. Except as permitted under the United States Copyright Act, no part of this publication may be reproduced or distributed in any form or by any means, or stored in a database or retrieval system, without prior written permission from the publisher.

Printed in the United States of America.

Send all inquiries to:
SRA/McGraw-Hill
8787 Orion Place
Columbus, OH 43240-4027

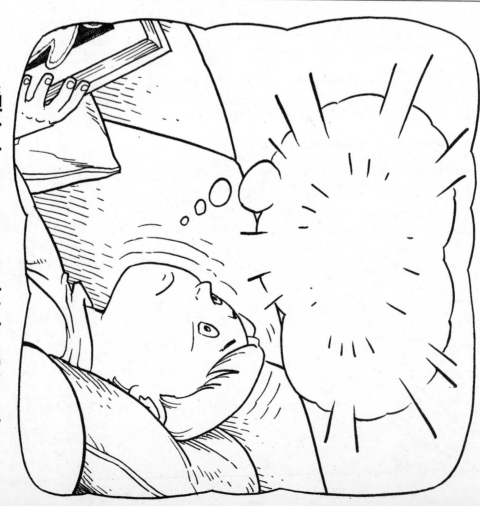

"This is strange," thinks Girard.
"Is this a magic place?
Am I awake?"

Girard was looking at pages.

3

"This is tragic," says the gingerbread man. "I do not like your thinking."

6

"Yum. I like gingerbread,"
thinks Girard.
"I wish I had some now."

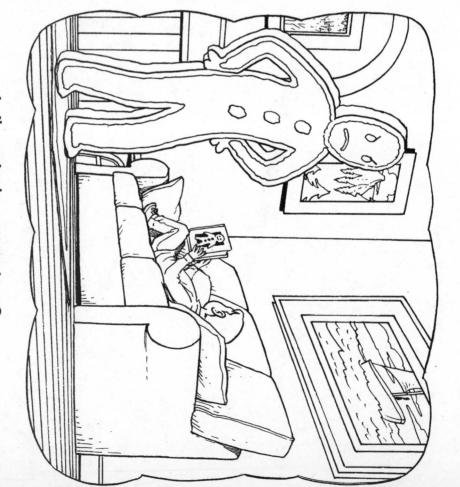

What is happening?
It is the gingerbread man.
Is he mad at Girard?
He looks agitated.

SRA Open Court Reading

No Regrets

by Jane Ward

illustrated by Deborah Colvin Borgo

Practice Book 60

SRA

A Division of The McGraw-Hill Companies

Columbus, Ohio

53

It is no secret. We have no regrets.
Edith and I like Princess a lot,
and she likes us a lot.

8

www.sra4kids.com

SRA/McGraw-Hill

A Division of The McGraw-Hill Companies

Copyright © 2002 by SRA/McGraw-Hill.

Printed in the United States of America.

Send all inquiries to:
SRA/McGraw-Hill
8787 Orion Place
Columbus, OH 43240-4027

2

We got a bed for her.
We got snacks for her.
We even got balls and bones for her.

7

Not too long ago, Edith and I got a good surprise.

3

She said, "Yes, but you must remember that Princess will depend on you."

6

My pal Jesse was going to a new
home far away.
He had to find a place for his
regal little dog, Princess.

4

Edith and I had an idea.
We asked Mom if we could give
Princess a home.

5

SRA Open Court Reading

The Play

by Bink Picard
illustrated by Pat Lucas-Morris

Practice Book 61

SRA
A Division of The McGraw-Hill Companies
Columbus, Ohio

Eve and Pete are a big hit.

8

www.sra4kids.com

SRA/McGraw-Hill

A Division of The McGraw-Hill Companies

Copyright © 2002 by SRA/McGraw-Hill.

Send all inquiries to:
SRA/McGraw-Hill
8787 Orion Place
Columbus, OH 43240-4027

Eve is acting with Pete.

Pete and Eve complete the play.

These belong to Eve.
Eve will use these.

3

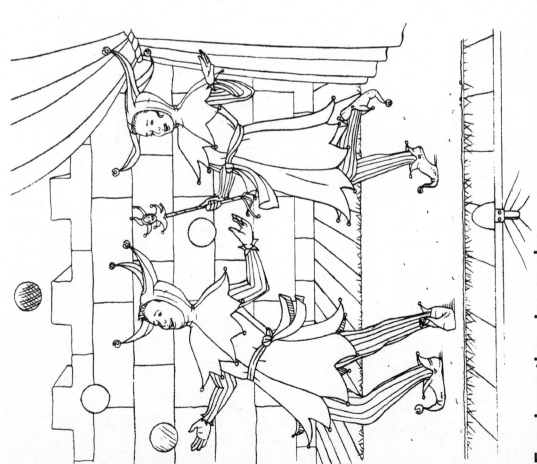

Eve is acting in a play.
The theme of the play is fun, fun, fun.

6

4

"Here, Eve," said Steve.
"These will make your
clothing complete."

"Thank you, Steve," said Eve.
"These make me look even better."

5

SRA Open Court Reading

I Can't Sleep

by Jill Foster
illustrated by Len Epstein

Practice Book 62

SRA

A Division of The McGraw-Hill Companies

Columbus, Ohio

Jeepers did think of sheep.
Lots and lots of sheep.
But still no rest for Jeepers.

61

8

www.sra4kids.com

SRA/McGraw-Hill

A Division of The McGraw-Hill Companies

Copyright © 2002 by SRA/McGraw-Hill.

Printed in the United States of America.

Send all inquiries to:
SRA/McGraw-Hill
8787 Orion Place
Columbus, OH 43240-4027

"Go back to your stall and think of sheep.
Think of sheep and you will fall asleep.
You will see."

Jeepers the steer is going to sleep.
He needs his sleep to feel good in
the morning.

3

Jeepers creeps from his stall to
seek help from his dad.
"Dad, I can't sleep."

6

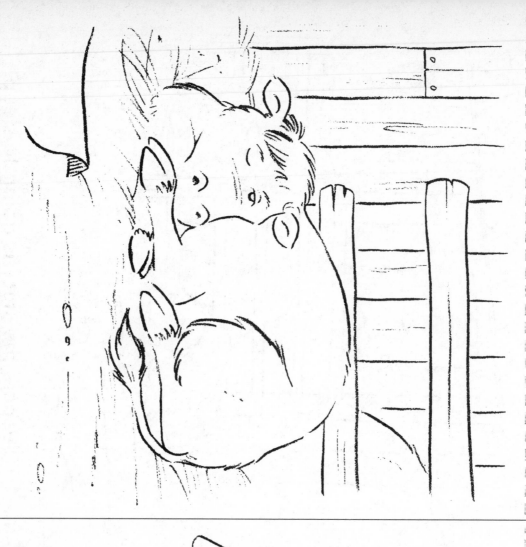

But Jeepers keeps peeking!
He just can't seem to fall asleep.

4

He is too cold.
He pulls his green sheet up to his cheek.
He is too hot.
He kicks the sheet off with his feet.

5

SRA OPEN COURT READING

The Clean Kitchen

by Carol Johnson
illustrated by Kersti Frigell

Practice Book 63

SRA

A Division of The McGraw-Hill Companies

Columbus, Ohio

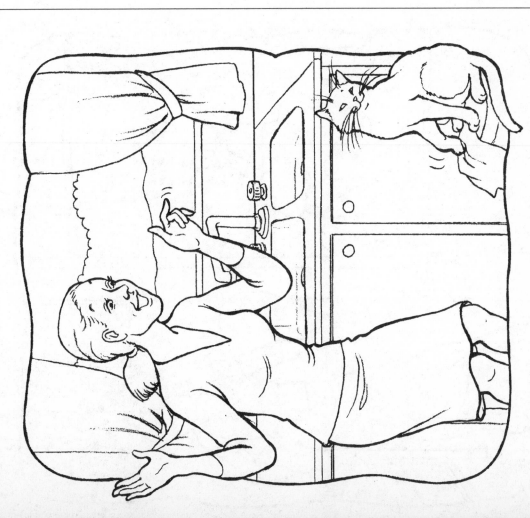

"Is this a dream? Whiskers, did
you clean up this kitchen?"

8

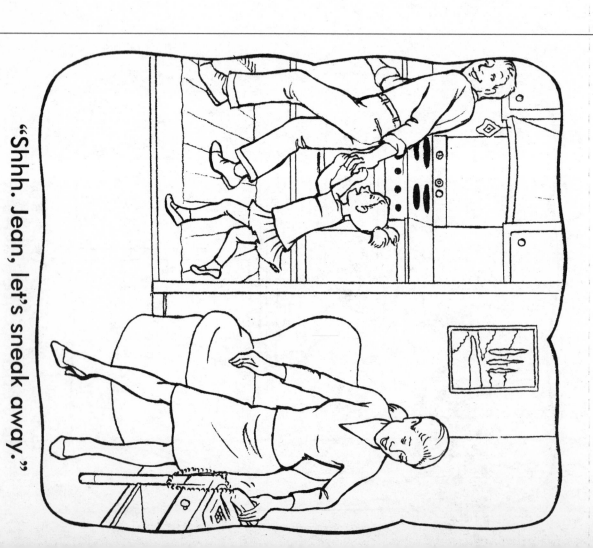

"Shhh. Jean, let's sneak away."

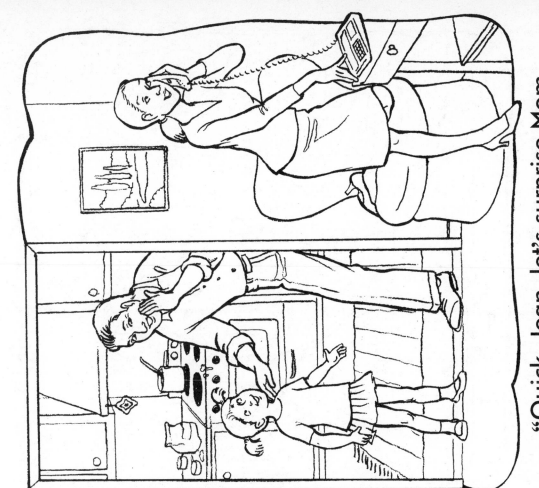

"Quick, Jean, let's surprise Mom
and clean up the kitchen."

3

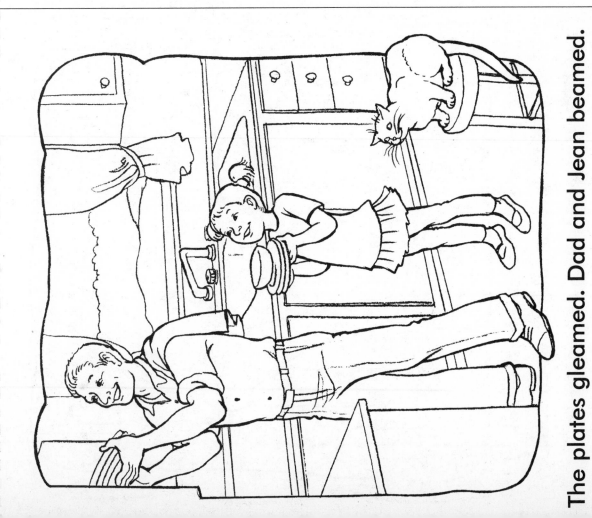

The plates gleamed. Dad and Jean beamed.

6

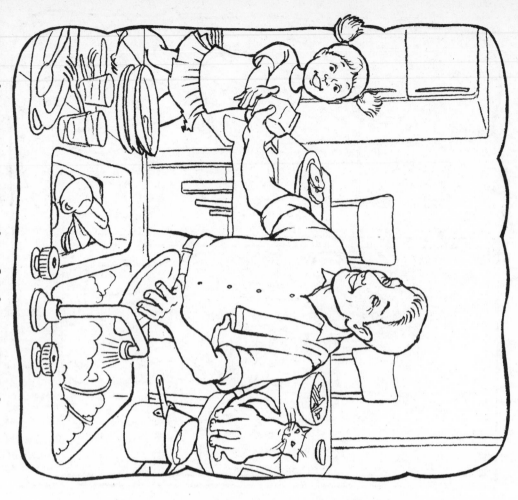

"Put the cream in the fridge. Quick, put the leftover beans and meat in, too."

4

The water streamed into the sink. Dad and Jean scrubbed each fork until it squeaked.

5

SRA Open Court Reading

The Smith City Cubs Win

by Dennis Fertig
illustrated by Meryl Henderson

Practice Book 64

A Division of The McGraw-Hill Companies

Columbus, Ohio

The Cubs, the children, and the city are happy.

8

www.sra4kids.com

SRA/McGraw-Hill

A Division of The McGraw-Hill Companies

Copyright © 2002 by SRA/McGraw-Hill.

Send all inquiries to:
SRA/McGraw-Hill
8787 Orion Place
Columbus, OH 43240-4027

Each child gets a copy of the shiny medal.
The children are happy.

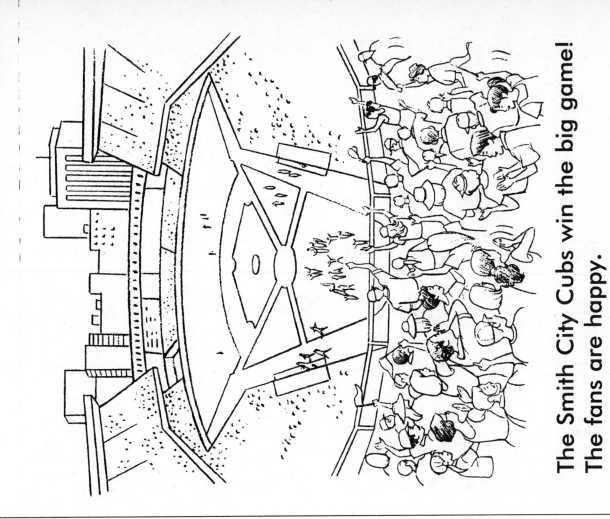

The Smith City Cubs win the big game!
The fans are happy.

3

Each Cub gets a shiny medal.
The Cubs are happy.

6

The city is happy.
There is a big parade and party.

Classes are canceled.
The children do not have to study.
The children hurry to see the
Smith City Cubs.

73

SRA Open Court Reading

The Game Pieces

by Beth Fintan
illustrated by Len Epstein

Practice Book 65

A Division of The McGraw-Hill Companies

Columbus, Ohio

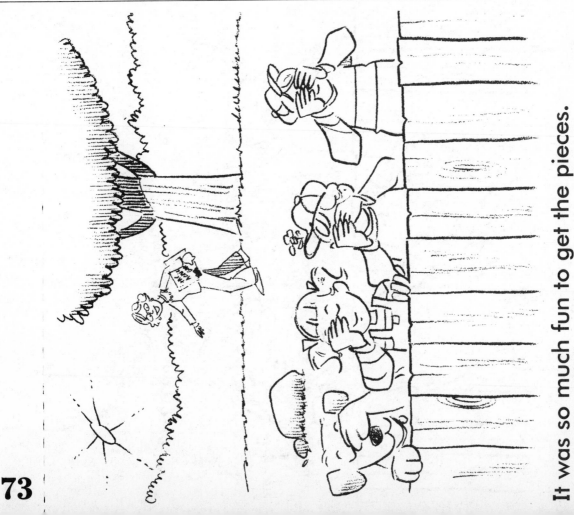

It was so much fun to get the pieces.
We will make a new game.
We can call it "Hide the Pieces in the Field."

8

www.sra4kids.com

SRA/McGraw-Hill

A Division of The McGraw-Hill Companies

Copyright © 2002 by SRA/McGraw-Hill.

All rights reserved. Except as permitted under the United States Copyright Act, no part of this publication may be reproduced or distributed in any form or by any means, or stored in a database or retrieval system, without prior written permission from the publisher.

Printed in the United States of America.

Send all inquiries to:
SRA/McGraw-Hill
8787 Orion Place
Columbus, OH 43240-4027

2

The cup was in the middle of the field.
I believe Walt stepped on it.

7

A hole is in the game box.
The game pieces fell out.
The pieces fell in this field.

3

This piece is a race car.
Nellie picked it up.
Nellie is my niece.

6

4

This piece is a chief's hat.
It was by the tree.
Jeff spotted it.

This piece is a shield.
It was by the rock.
Mollie the dog helped find this piece.

5

The Train

SRA Open Court Reading

by Anne Walsh
illustrated by Meryl Henderson

Practice Book 66

SRA

A Division of The McGraw-Hill Companies

Columbus, Ohio

The train stopped running
when I was six.
I still miss hearing the faint
rumble of the train.

www.sra4kids.com

SRA/McGraw-Hill

A Division of The McGraw-Hill Companies

Copyright © 2002 by SRA/McGraw-Hill.

Printed in the United States of America.

Send all inquiries to:
SRA/McGraw-Hill
8787 Orion Place
Columbus, OH 43240-4027

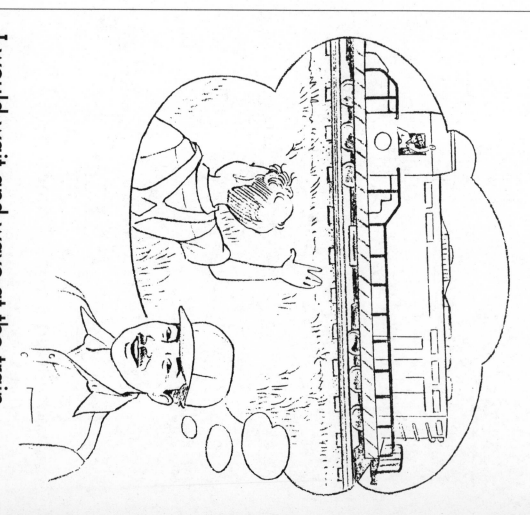

I would wait and wave at the train.
The engineer on the train would wave back.

When I was five, a train ran past this field.
The main track was up on the hill.

3

The train had sacks of mail.
It gained speed from the quaint, little city
to the big city.
It made the trip daily, rain or shine.

6

Under the daisies, you can see
the remains of the track.
The rails are made of steel. The
rails now make a trail.

The train had plainly painted cars.
The cars were filled with grain.
The train went from the farms to a
quaint, little city.
The horn wailed. It never failed.

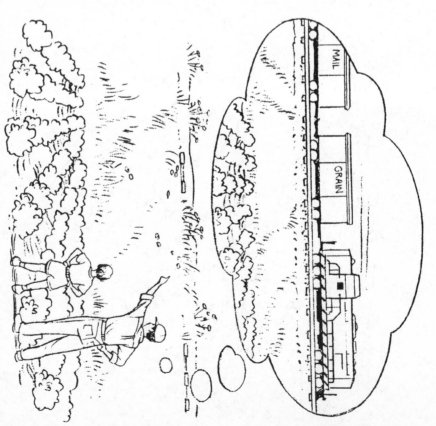

SRA OPEN COURT READING

A Gray, Rainy Day

by Dennis Fertig
illustrated by Kersti Frigell

Practice Book 67

SRA

A Division of The McGraw-Hill Companies

Columbus, Ohio

81

"I will play," said Jay.

"It is the best thing to do when it is rainy and gray."

8

2

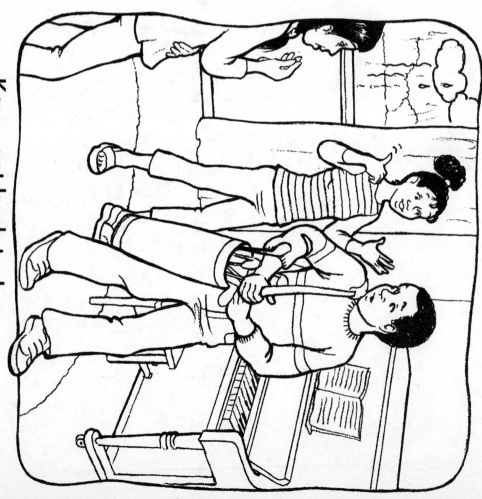

Kay went back to Jay.
"It is not sunny," said Kay.
"It is gray and rainy!" said Jay.

7

83

Kay set up the gray painting.
She turned on the hose.
It sprayed.

6

"Will you play music for us?" asked Kay.
"It is a sunny day," said Jay.
"I will do it on a gray and rainy day."

3

4

Kay liked Jay to play.
She had a plan.
Kay had a way to make Jay play.

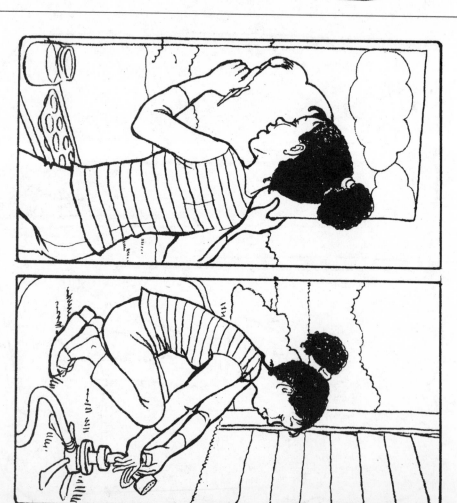

5

Kay made a gray painting.
Then Kay fixed the hose.
She set it to spray.

City Lights at Night

SRA Open Court Reading

by Beth Fintan
illustrated by Meryl Henderson

Practice Book 68

SRA

A Division of The McGraw-Hill Companies

Columbus, Ohio

85

We like to sail at night. Dad makes the rope tight.
We might go sailing next on Sunday night.

www.sra4kids.com

SRA/McGraw-Hill

A Division of The McGraw-Hill Companies

Copyright © 2002 by SRA/McGraw-Hill.

Printed in the United States of America.

Send all inquiries to:
SRA/McGraw-Hill
8787 Orion Place
Columbus, OH 43240-4027

2

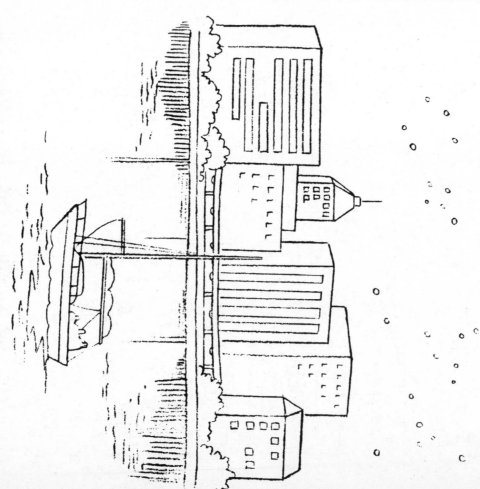

The bright city lights glitter.
The bright city lights glitter in the lake, too.
The city lights are quite a sight.

7

86

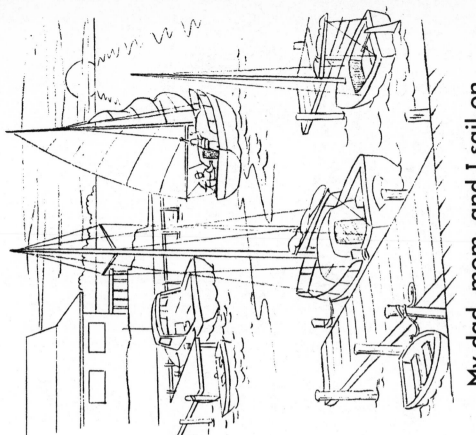

My dad, mom, and I sail on
the lake Friday night.
We sail on nice nights to see
the city lights.

3

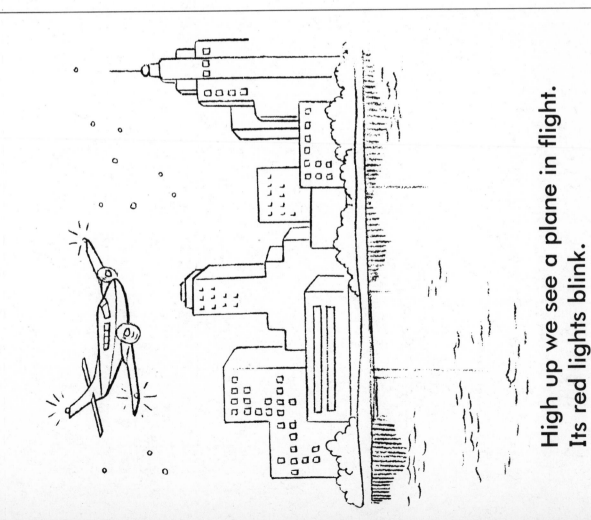

High up we see a plane in flight.
Its red lights blink.

6

We start right by the bright lights
in the city.
A slight wind takes us out.

4

We sigh when we see
the city from the lake.
The lights sparkle at night.

5

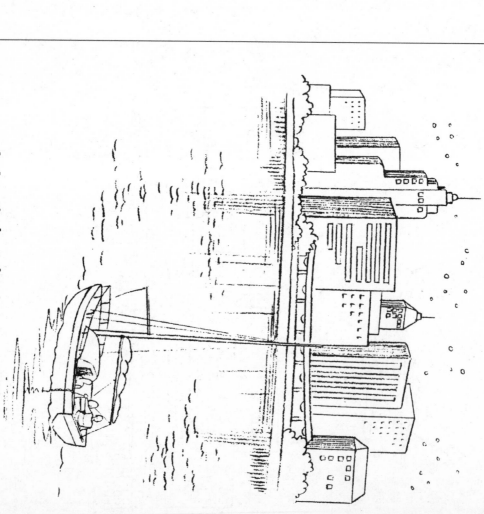

SRA Open Court Reading

Sly and Ty

by Anton Vanerka
illustrated by Len Epstein

Practice Book 69

SRA

A Division of The McGraw-Hill Companies

Columbus, Ohio

"This is a nice way to rest," said Sly.
"It is the best way to fly," added Ty.

www.sra4kids.com

SRA/McGraw-Hill

A Division of The McGraw-Hill Companies

Copyright © 2002 by SRA/McGraw-Hill.

All rights reserved. Except as permitted under the United States Copyright Act, no part of this publication may be reproduced or distributed in any form or by any means, or stored in a database or retrieval system, without prior written permission from the publisher.

Printed in the United States of America.

Send all inquiries to:
SRA/McGraw-Hill
8787 Orion Place
Columbus, OH 43240-4027

2

Sly and Ty dove down and landed on the wing.
"We did it on the first try," said Sly.

7

Sly and Ty were high in the sky.
"My wings are tired," sighed Sly.
"My wings are so tired I might cry," Ty added.

3

"Let's try to catch up to the plane," said Ty.
"Why?" asked Sly.
Ty gave his reply: "Just try and you will see."

6

4

"Why not rest?" asked Sly.
"We have too far to fly," said Ty.

Then a plane went by.

5

SRA Open Court Reading

The Best Pie

by Dennis Fertig
illustrated by Len Epstein

Practice Book 70

SRA
A Division of The McGraw-Hill Companies
Columbus, Ohio

I like each pie best.
It is a tie!

Which pie do I like best?
I cannot lie.

95

Which pie do I like best?
Let me try the peach pie.

3

I cannot lie.
I like the lemon pie.

6

4

I cannot lie.
I like the peach pie.

Which pie do I like best?
Let me try the lemon pie.

5

SRA OPEN COURT READING

Joe and His Oboe

by Alice Henderson
illustrated by Jan Pyk

Practice Book 71

A Division of The McGraw-Hill Companies

Columbus, Ohio

Joe uses his oboe to get rid of the doe.

8

2

Joe goes inside to get his oboe.

7

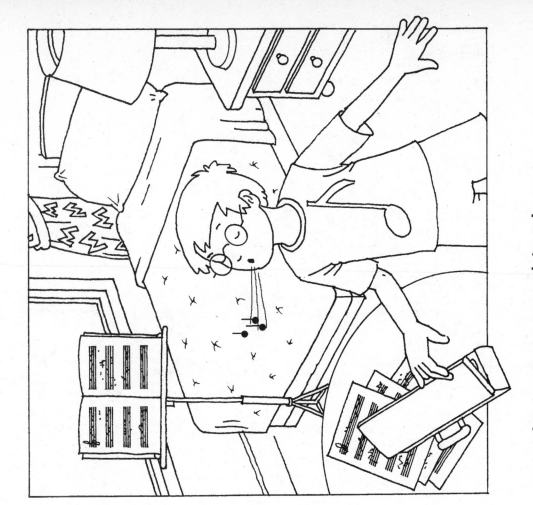

Joe puts away his oboe.
It is time to help in the garden.

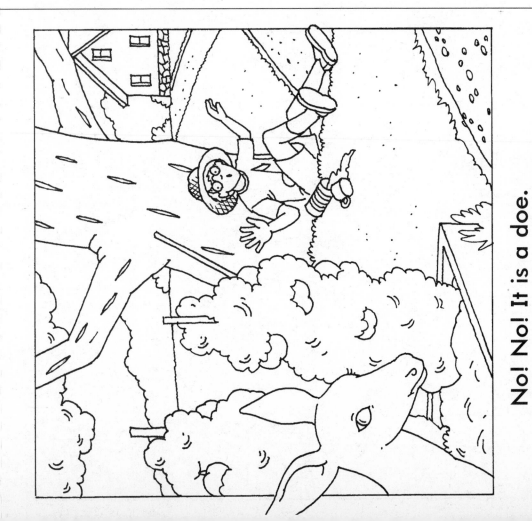

No! No! It is a doe.
She is a foe in a garden.
She is eating the plants.

6

Joe takes his hoe to get rid of the weeds.
Joe hoes and hoes until he is hot and tired.

4

Joe sits down for a rest.
What is that Joe sees in the garden?

5

SRA OPEN COURT READING

Joan's Boat

by Mitch Jenkins
illustrated by Jan Pyk

Practice Book 72

SRA

A Division of The McGraw-Hill Companies

Columbus, Ohio

But Joan forgot about her soap!
Joan groans, "If only soapy dishes
were as fun as a boat."

8

www.sra4kids.com

SRA/McGraw-Hill

A Division of The McGraw-Hill Companies

Copyright © 2002 by SRA/McGraw-Hill.

Printed in the United States of America.

Send all inquiries to:
SRA/McGraw-Hill
8787 Orion Place
Columbus, OH 43240-4027

She floats in the waves.
She soaks up the hot sun.

The soap foams in the sink.

3

Joan dreams she sails her boat up
and down the coast.

9

103

One of the oatmeal dishes floats.

4

The dish makes Joan think of a boat.
Joan's mind begins to roam.

5

Sam and Dad Bowl

by Clarence Williams
illustrated by Barry Mullins

Practice Book 73

SRA

A Division of The McGraw-Hill Companies

Columbus, Ohio

Dad's smile glowed. "See, Sam, I told you I'd show you the right way to bowl."

www.sra4kids.com

SRA/McGraw-Hill

A Division of The McGraw-Hill Companies

Copyright © 2002 by SRA/McGraw-Hill.

Printed in the United States of America.

Send all inquiries to:
SRA/McGraw-Hill
8787 Orion Place
Columbus, OH 43240-4027

Dad followed Sam.
Dad slowed down.
Dad bent his elbow.
Dad's ball hit every pin!

Sam and Dad go bowling.

3

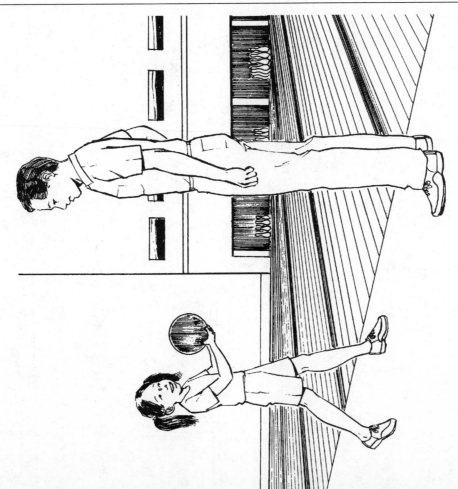

Sam followed Dad.
"Look, Dad. Try to slow down.
Bend your elbow, and let the ball go low."

6

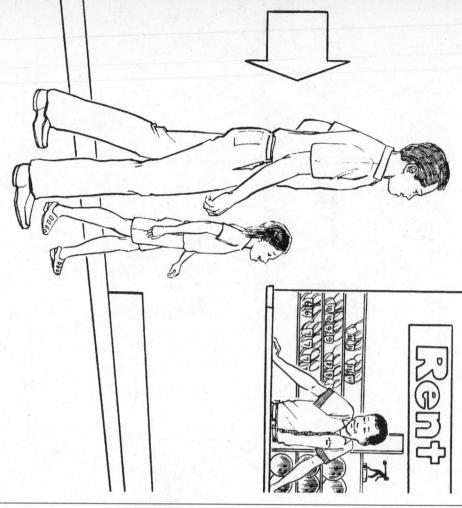

Sam and Dad don't own bowling balls.
Sam and Dad will rent them.
A big red arrow shows them where to go.

4

Dad says, "I'll show you the right way
to bowl."
But Dad's ball rolls off the narrow lane.

5

SRA OPEN COURT READING

Dad's Chair

by Cathy Jensen
illustrated by Barry Mullins

Practice Book 74

SRA
A Division of The McGraw-Hill Companies
Columbus, Ohio

Lucky Tip!
Few cats get to lie in a handmade chair!

8

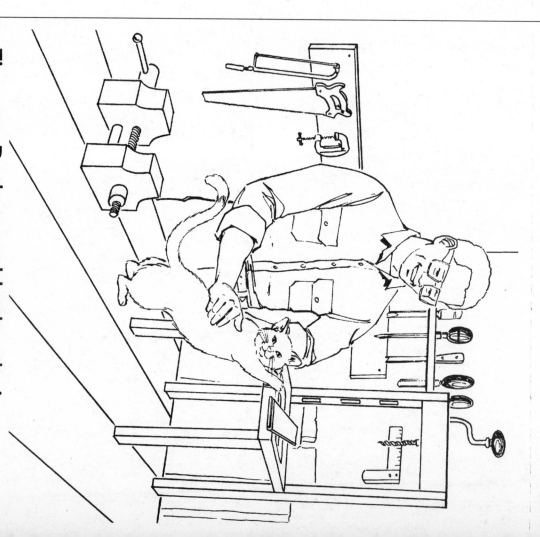

Tip sees Dad assemble the chair.
Tip mews and Dad takes time to pet her.

This is a yew tree.

3

Few men can make a chair from a yew tree like Dad can.

6

First Dad will hew, or cut down, the yew tree.
Then he will create a chair from the tree.

4

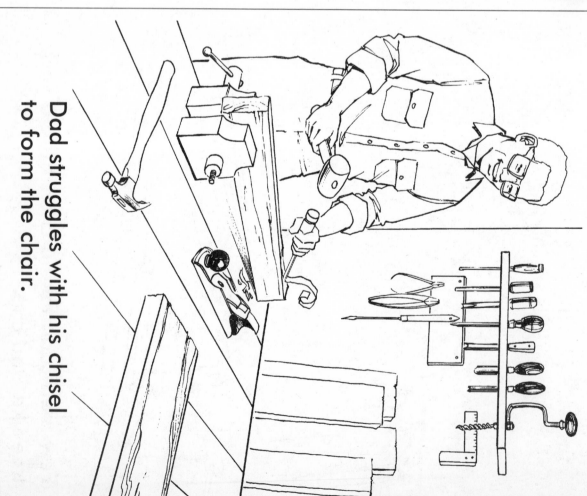

Dad struggles with his chisel
to form the chair.

5

SRA Open Court Reading

Mark's Dream

by Jill Rodgers
illustrated by Kersti Frigell

Practice Book 75

A Division of The McGraw-Hill Companies

Columbus, Ohio

The catalog continues to supply useful camping tips.
It seems that the only tip it does not give is how to get parents to go camping!

8

Mark even sees a tip on how to get help for a rescue.
No one can argue with a good tip for getting help quickly and safely.

It is Mark's dream to go camping.
Mark is reading a catalog called
Camper's Best Pal.

3

115

The next hint tells about using sticks and
dried grass for fuel.
It suggests ways to carry them in a tote.
That's a big help.

6

4

There are lots of helpful hints in this catalog. Mark understands the value of being prepared.

The first hint is a yummy one. It tells how to fix barbecued ribs on a camp stove. His parents will like that.

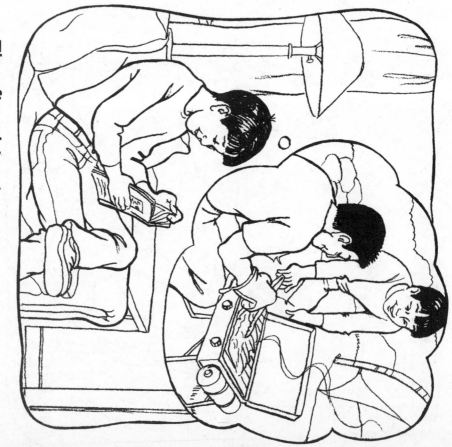

5

SRA Open Court Reading

Jayce Helps

by John Murphy
illustrated by Olivia Cole

Practice Book 76

SRA

A Division of The McGraw-Hill Companies
Columbus, Ohio

117

"What happened, Jayce?"
"Amy was droopy, so I tried
to perk her up."

8

Amy is gloomy.
Her mood is quite bad.

7

Mom sits on a stool in the garden and makes rows for seeds.
Jayce holds a tray with Mom's tools.

3

119

Jayce's big sister Amy zoomed past with an airplane.
She made the plane swoop, dive, and loop the loop.
Mom said, "We will go in for lunch soon. It is almost noon. Put the plane away."

6

"See, Jayce, just put a little dirt over the seeds to give the tender shoots room to grow. In a while, the roots will be strong, and plants will bloom."

"See these smooth starts, Jayce? They are droopy. Spray them with water to perk them up."

5

SRA
OPEN COURT
READING

A Bluebird for Sue

by Rebecca Blankenhorn
illustrated by Olivia Cole

Practice Book 77

SRA

A Division of The McGraw-Hill Companies

Columbus, Ohio

121

It is true!
Sue has a bluebird
that she can keep.

www.sra4kids.com

SRA/McGraw-Hill

A Division of The McGraw-Hill Companies

Copyright © 2002 by SRA/McGraw-Hill.

Printed in the United States of America.

Send all inquiries to:
SRA/McGraw-Hill
8787 Orion Place
Columbus, OH 43240-4027

Sue will make a bluebird!
She glues small, blue pom-poms.
She glues yellow felt for feet and a beak.
She glues blue felt for wings and a tail.

123

Sue sees bluebirds on Grand Avenue.
The bluebirds make a nest in an old tree.

3

After five weeks, the baby bluebird can fly.
Then the bluebirds go away from Grand Avenue. Sue is sad.
Sue misses the bluebirds.
She needs a bluebird that will stay.

6

Sue sees an egg in the nest.
The egg has a crack. Sue thinks it is a clue.
The egg is due to hatch.

4

Here is the baby bluebird with its mom and dad.
Sue likes the bluebirds. She visits the birds on Grand Avenue each day.

5

SRA
Open Court
Reading

What Tune?

by Dennis Fertig
illustrated by Deborah Colvin Borgo

Practice Book 78

SRA

A Division of The McGraw-Hill Companies

Columbus, Ohio

125

"I feel bad," said June.

8

"June," said Big Sam.
"I see where the tune is.
It is on your neck."

www.sra4kids.com

SRA/McGraw-Hill
A Division of The McGraw-Hill Companies

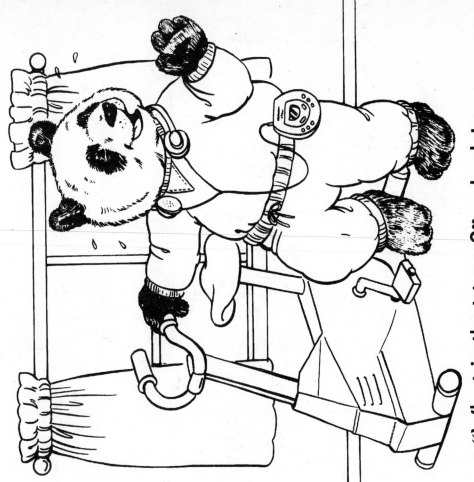

"What is that tune?" asked June.

"It is rude to play a tune this late."

"Big Sam, are you playing the flute?" yelled June.

3

"No, I am not playing a tube tune," replied Little Sam.

"It is rude to play this late. I am reading."

6

"No," replied Big Sam.
"I am not playing my flute. I make it
a rule not to play this late."

4

"What is that tune?" asked June.
"Little Sam," yelled June.
"Did you make a horn from a tube?"

5

SRA OPEN COURT READING

A Space Crew

by Ross Budka
illustrated by Meryl Henderson

Practice Book 79

SRA

A Division of The McGraw-Hill Companies

Columbus, Ohio

The shuttle landed.
The crew is safe and happy.
A new crew and shuttle will
fly next May or June.

8

The crew had space meals.
They wished for homemade stew.
The crew liked brewed tea.

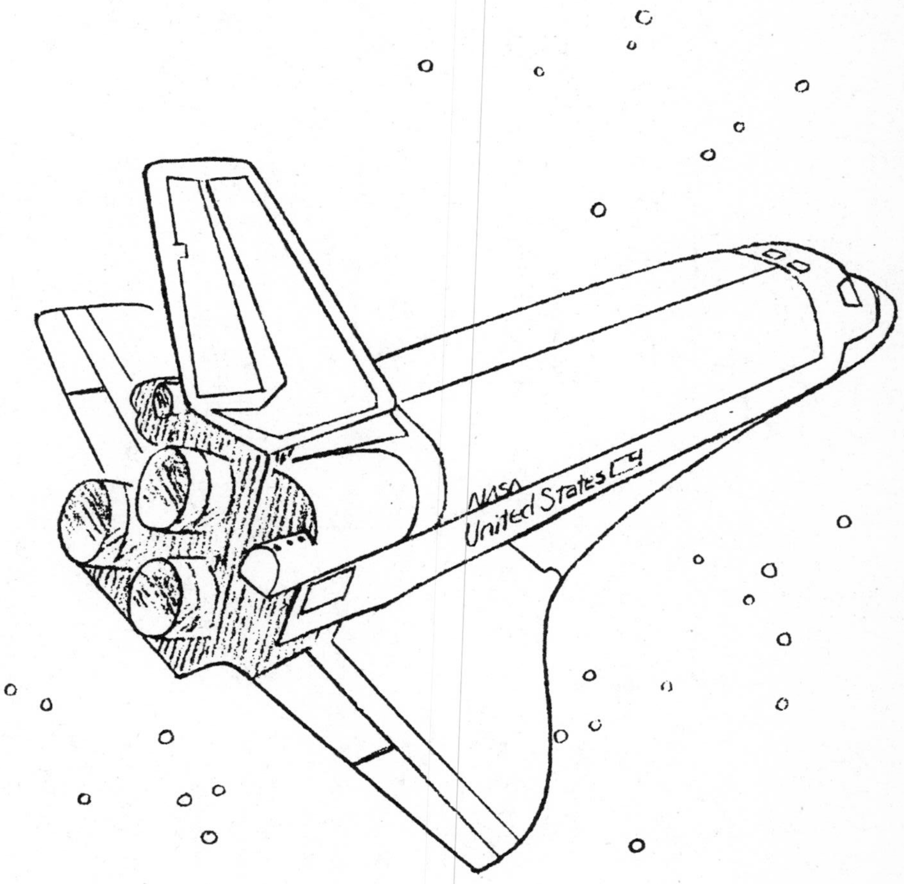

A new crew flew in the space shuttle.
The space shuttle flew high in the dark sky.

3

A wire blew off the shuttle.
The crew walked in space.
They screwed on a new wire.

6

The shuttle crew worked hard.
The shuttle stayed in space for weeks.

4

The pets chewed on the plants.
They grew plants and fed pets.
The crew did tests in space.

5

SRA Open Court Reading

Ruth and Ruby

by Dennis Fertig
illustrated by Kersti Frigell

Practice Book 80

SRA

A Division of The McGraw-Hill Companies

Columbus, Ohio

What do Ruby and Ruth both like?
The truth is not much.
But both like having a twin sister.

8

133

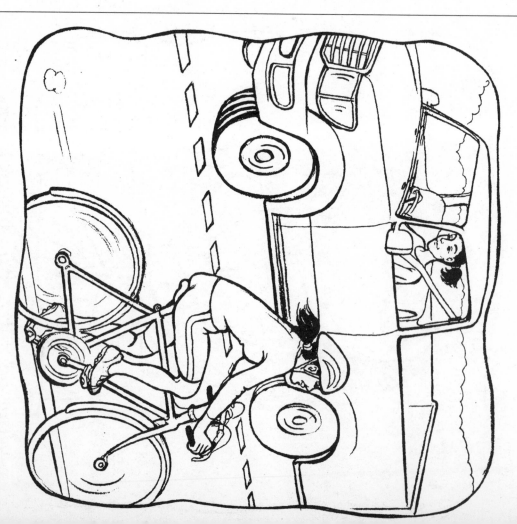

Ruby likes to drive a heavy-duty truck.
Ruth is happy on her bike.

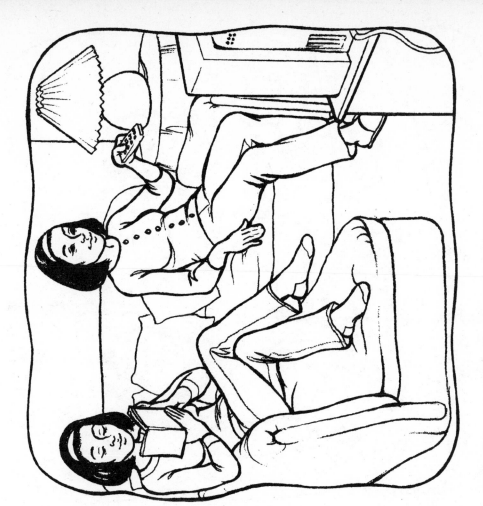

Ruth and Ruby are twins.
Some twins like the same things.
The truth is that Ruth and Ruby do not.

3

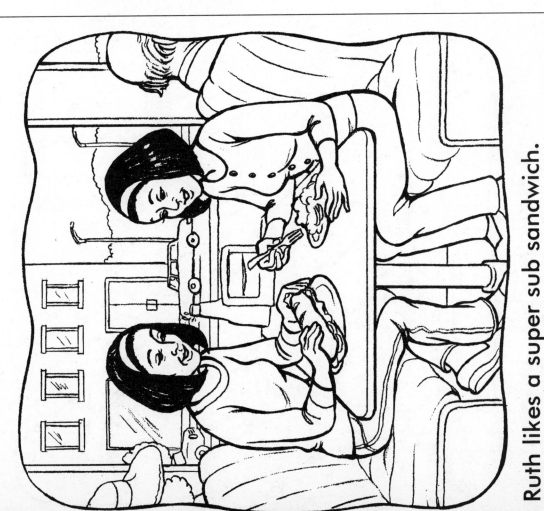

Ruth likes a super sub sandwich.
A super sub sandwich is too big for Ruby.

6

Ruth likes tuna.
Ruby cannot stand tuna.

Ruby likes summer days in June.
Ruth likes winter.

137

SRA Open Court Reading

The Best Cook

by Anne Walsh

illustrated by Kersti Frigell

Practice Book 81

SRA

A Division of The McGraw-Hill Companies

Columbus, Ohio

Mom saves cooking tips in a wooden box.

Dad saves cooking tips in his head.

Mom is a good cook, but Dad is the best.

8

2

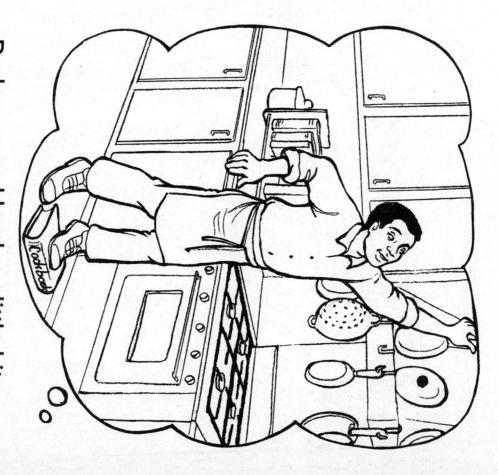

Dad uses cookbooks a little bit.
Last night, he stood on a cookbook
to get a pan from a hook.

7

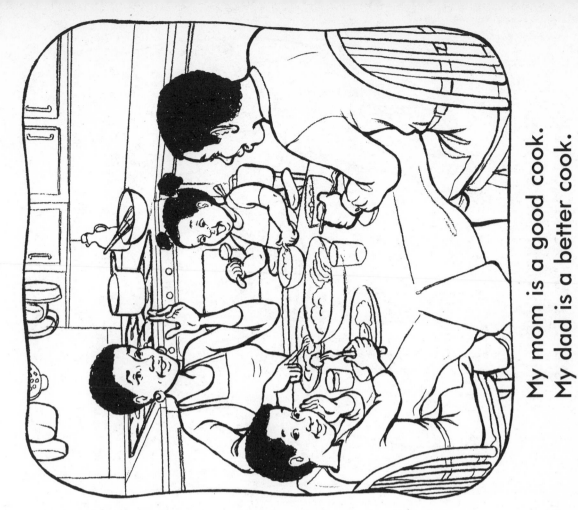

My mom is a good cook.
My dad is a better cook.

3

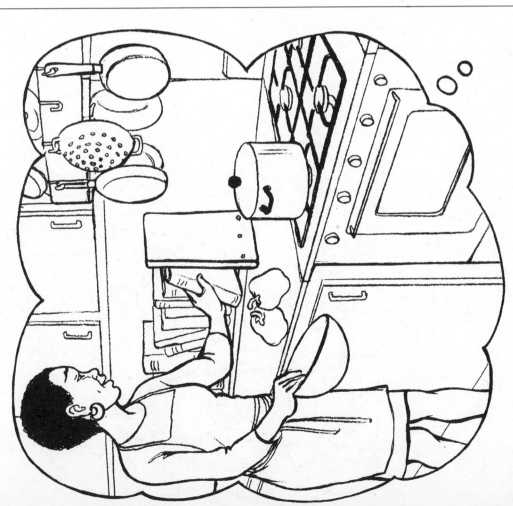

139

Mom has lots of cookbooks.
She made a wooden bookcase for them.

6

4

Mom works hard at cooking.
She took cooking lessons.

Dad never took cooking lessons.
He has cooked all his life.

5

Maggy's Flower

SRA Open Court Reading

by Alex Gonzalez
illustrated by Shawn McManus

Practice Book 82

SRA

A Division of The McGraw-Hill Companies

Columbus, Ohio

141

Maggy is allowed to keep her flower.
The flower makes Maggy happy, and when
Maggy is happy, she plows.

2

Maggy stops her plow.

7

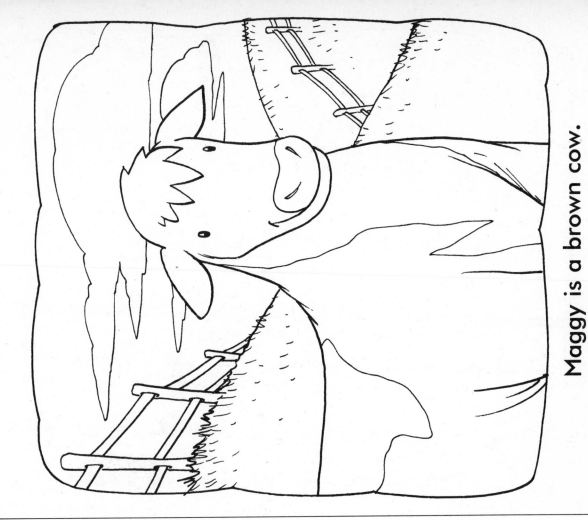

3

Maggy is a brown cow.

Maggy sees a lonely flower.
Maggy frowns. Maggy scowls.

6

Maggy is big and powerful.
She is the most powerful cow in town.

4

Maggy plows.
The farmer's pals are amazed
at how well Maggy plows.

5

SRA Open Court Reading

Nicky Gets a Hit

by Rick Powers
illustrated by Meryl Henderson

Practice Book 83

SRA
A Division of The McGraw-Hill Companies
Columbus, Ohio

Nicky hit a home run!
She bounds around the bases.
The loud shouts do not bother her now!

8

Nicky stepped back.
She took a deep breath.
She told herself, "I will not get out.
I will pound the ball up to the clouds."

7

146

Nicky sat in the dugout.
Coach shouted, "Nicky, it's your turn
to bat. We are counting on you."

3

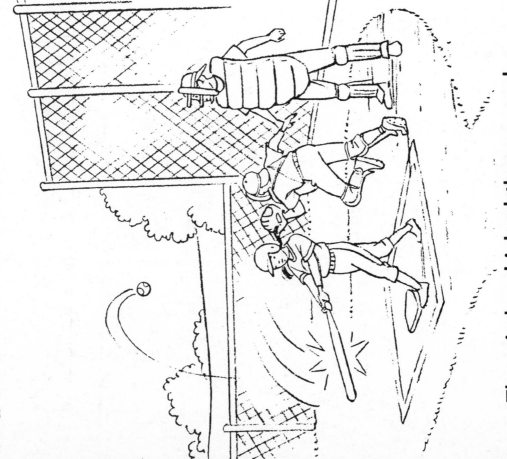

The pitcher kicked the ground
and threw again.
Nicky hit a foul.

6

Nicky looked around.
The crowd sounded very loud.
Nicky was a little jumpy.

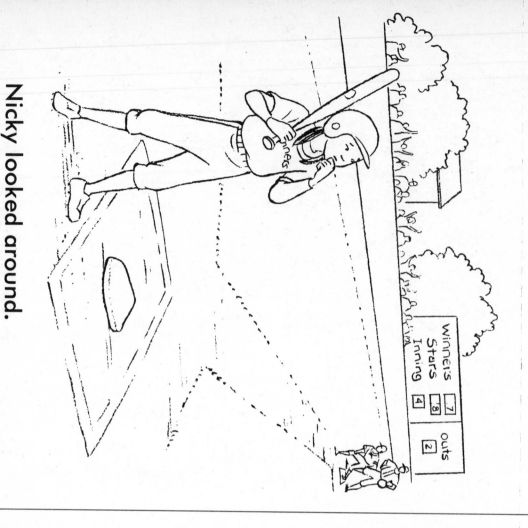

The pitcher on the mound threw the ball.
Nicky swung and missed.

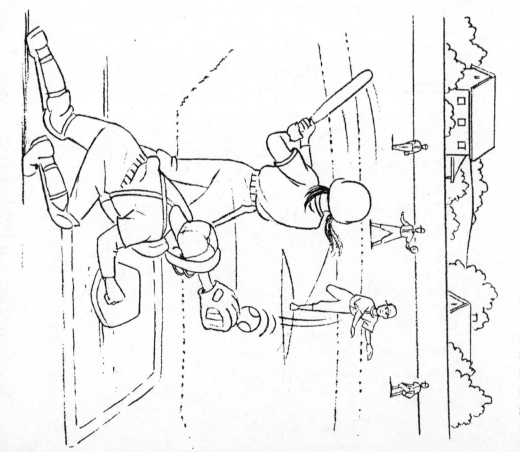

SRA Open Court Reading

Too Much Help

by Tracy Philips
illustrated by Len Epstein

Practice Book 84

SRA

A Division of The McGraw-Hill Companies
Columbus, Ohio

149

"I'm fine," Mom replied. "I was going to take you to the astronaut museum next, but I am afraid. The way things are going you might get launched right into space. Maybe we will go a different day."

8

www.sra4kids.com

SRA/McGraw-Hill

A Division of The McGraw-Hill Companies

Send all inquiries to:
SRA/McGraw-Hill
8787 Orion Place
Columbus, OH 43240-4027

2

When they got back to the auto, Mom looked quite tired.

"Are you all right?" Austin and Paula asked.

On a hot August day, Mom hauled Austin and Paula in her auto. They had jobs to do.

3

When Paula picked up the eggs, they slipped out of her hands. What a mess!

"It's okay," the owner said. "It is not your fault."

6

First Austin and Paula helped
Mom do laundry.
Austin bumped into a faucet and
water went all over.

4

Then Austin, Paula, and Mom went
to the grocery.
Austin asked for applesauce.
Paula asked for cauliflower.
Mom needed flour, milk, and eggs.

5

SRA Open Court Reading

Awful the Hawk

by Dillon Brown
illustrated by Shawn McManus

Practice Book 85

SRA

A Division of The McGraw-Hill Companies

Columbus, Ohio

153

Awful is not awful to Chip.
Awful and Chip are pals!
"Put your paws around my leg,"
squawks Awful.
"I saw a super place for breakfast."

8

2

Chip yawns and stretches.
He is not afraid of Awful's claws.

7

Awful the hawk gets up too soon.
She gets up way too soon.
In fact, Awful the hawk awakes
and squawks at dawn.

3

Then just after dawn, Awful stops by.
She has a powerful jaw and awfully
sharp claws.
Awful tries to wake Chip.

6

4

She yawns and stretches her claws.
What will Awful have for breakfast?

At dawn Chip is sprawled
out on some straw.
Chip is still asleep.

5

SRA OPEN COURT READING

Grammy's Knot

by Alice Burns
illustrated by Barry Mullins

Practice Book 86

SRA

A Division of The McGraw-Hill Companies

Columbus, Ohio

Grammy fixes Nate's knuckle.
Nate fixes Grammy's knot.

8

2

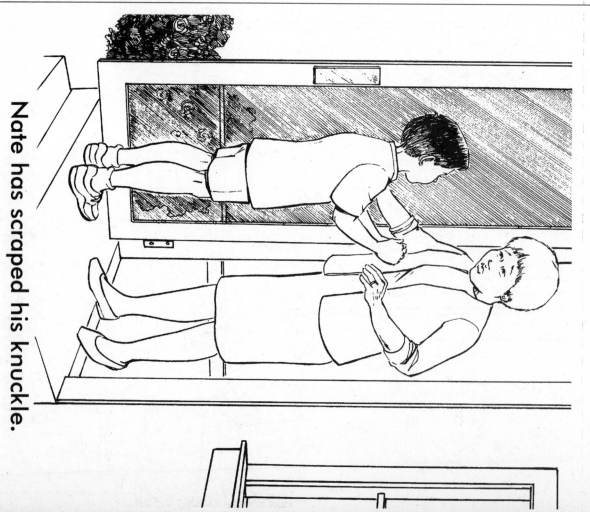

Nate has scraped his knuckle.

7

Grammy sits and knits.
The yarn is on her knees.

3

Nate knocks.

6

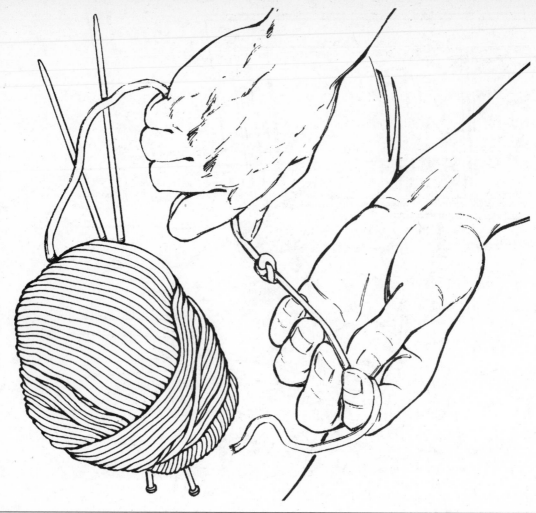

4

Grammy gets a knot in her knitting.

Grammy knows how to knit, but Grammy does not know how to get out this knot.

5

Open Court Reading

Cooking Supper

by Michael Peter
illustrated by Loretta Lustig

Practice Book 87

SRA

A Division of The McGraw-Hill Companies

Columbus, Ohio

Grammy and Gramps helped, too.
Grammy put foil on the leftovers so
they would not spoil.
And Gramps put them away.

8

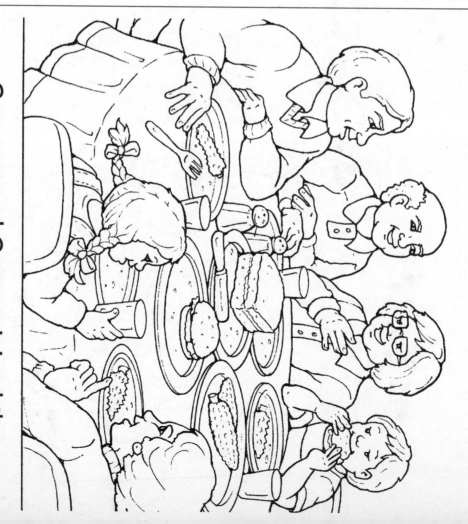

Grammy and Gramps joined the Smiths for supper.
No one was disappointed.
Everything was tasty.

The children had no choice.
It was something they could not avoid.
At the Smith home, everyone helped
with supper.

3

A voice called from the family
room. It was Mom.
"I will make a moist cake,"
she said.

6

4

Dad flipped a coin.
He pointed to Lester.
"Lester will help me boil corn
and broil hamburgers."

Then he pointed to Kate.
"Kate can make salad dressing
with this oil."

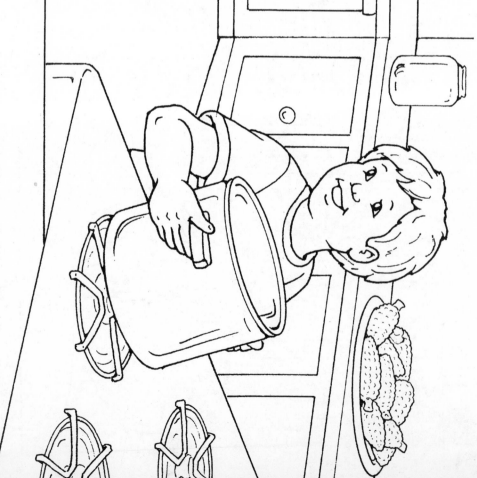

5

Open Court Reading

Joy's Jobs

by Michael Kryst
illustrated by Kersti Frigell

Practice Book 88

SRA

A Division of The McGraw-Hill Companies

Columbus, Ohio

165

Joy's daydream is over.
"What will I be?" Joy thinks.
"There are so many choices."
Don't get annoyed, Joy. You have
a long time to think about it.
Now, it is time for bed.

8

2

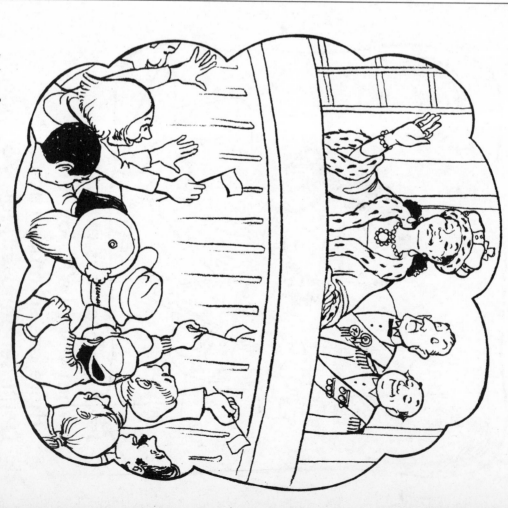

Maybe Joy can be a royal queen and have many loyal subjects.

7

167

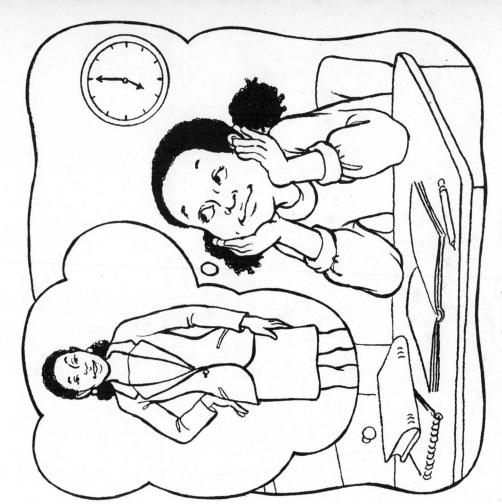

Joy enjoys daydreaming.
This day she is dreaming of what
she wants to be when she grows up.

3

Joy can see herself as an arctic explorer.
She will lead a convoy across miles and
miles of snow.

6

Perhaps she will own a toy shop.
She can employ her pal Troy.

4

Or maybe she will be an oyster diver.

5

Thank-You Note

SRA Open Court Reading

by Mike Gretchen
illustrated by Olivia Cole

Practice Book 89

SRA

A Division of The McGraw-Hill Companies

Columbus, Ohio

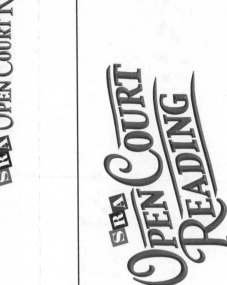

www.sra4kids.com

SRA/McGraw-Hill

A Division of The McGraw-Hill Companies

Copyright © 2002 by SRA/McGraw-Hill.

All rights reserved. Except as permitted under the United States Copyright Act, no part of this publication may be reproduced or distributed in any form or by any means, or stored in a database or retrieval system, without prior written permission from the publisher.

Printed in the United States of America.

Send all inquiries to:
SRA/McGraw-Hill
8787 Orion Place
Columbus, OH 43240-4027

2

Jill rewrote the note.
She used her best handwriting.

7

Jill was excited about the birthday gift.
It was from her Grammy.
The paper had a wrinkle in it from
being mailed.

3

Jill wrote a first draft.
"Mom, will you check my spelling?" Jill asked.
"I don't want to spell anything wrong."

6

4

The wrinkle didn't matter.
Jill unwrapped her gift quickly.
It was a new wristwatch!
And it had an alarm that sounded
like a wren singing.

Mom told Jill to write a
thank-you note to Grammy.
Jill started right away.
She hadn't written to
Grammy in a long time.

Dear Grammy,
Thank you very much

Thank you

5

173

SRA Open Court Reading

Jobs in the World

by Emery Stoghoff
illustrated by Gary Undercuffler

Practice Book 90

SRA

A Division of The McGraw-Hill Companies

Columbus, Ohio

There are many jobs in the world:
mayors, sailors, tailors, and more.

8

www.sra4kids.com

SRA/McGraw-Hill

A Division of The McGraw-Hill Companies

Copyright © 2002 by SRA/McGraw-Hill.

All rights reserved. Except as permitted under the United States Copyright Act, no part of this publication may be reproduced or distributed in any form or by any means, or stored in a database or retrieval system, without prior written permission from the publisher.

Printed in the United States of America.

Send all inquiries to:
SRA/McGraw-Hill
8787 Orion Place
Columbus, OH 43240-4027

2

Jan's sister is an author.
She writes books with humor in them.

7

There are many jobs in the world.
Chuck's mom is a doctor.
She works in a hospital.

3

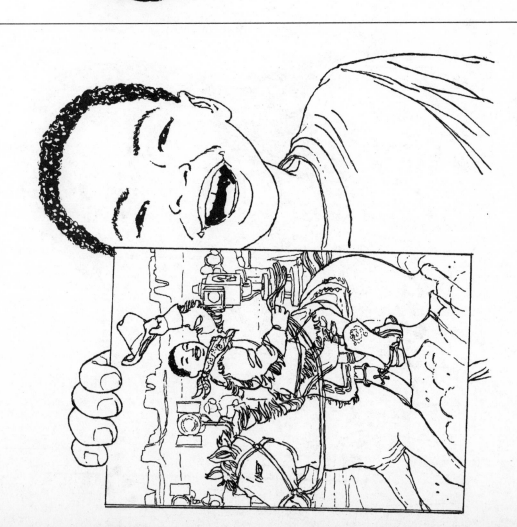

Howie has an uncle who is an actor.
Howie's uncle has a challenging job.

6

Gretchen's dad likes to work with colors.
He is an artist. He is good at his work.

Sally's gramps is a train conductor.
He travels lots of miles every day.

4

5

SRA Open Court Reading

Edgar

by Michael P. Fertig
illustrated by Deborah Colvin Borgo

Practice Book 91

SRA

A Division of The McGraw-Hill Companies

Columbus, Ohio

David loves Edgar.
Edgar is a spectacular dog.

8

www.sra4kids.com

SRA/McGraw-Hill

A Division of The McGraw-Hill Companies

Copyright © 2002 by SRA/McGraw-Hill.

All rights reserved. Except as permitted under the United States Copyright Act, no part of this publication may be reproduced or distributed in any form or by any means, or stored in a database or retrieval system, without prior written permission from the publisher.

Printed in the United States of America.

Send all inquiries to:
SRA/McGraw-Hill
8787 Orion Place
Columbus, OH 43240-4027

2

Edgar thinks he protects the family by chasing away spiders and caterpillars.

7

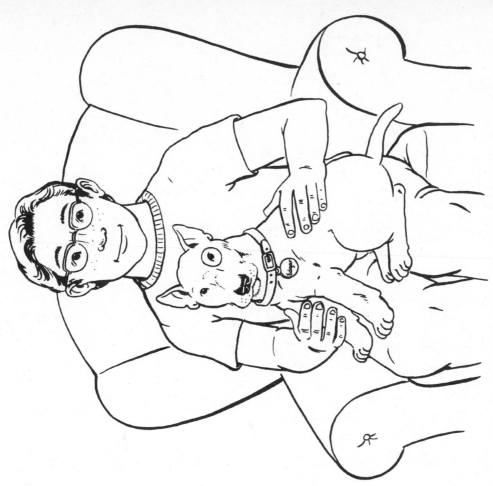

Edgar is the name of David's dog.
Edgar is a muscular dog.
David and Edgar look similar.

3

Edgar sleeps in the shade near
the cellar entryway.

6

Edgar is not a beggar, like some dogs. David feeds Edgar doggy treats that have a cheddar cheese flavor.

4

David got Edgar a new collar. It cost only a dollar.

5

SRA Open Court Reading

The Phantom Frog

by Irene Belnik
illustrated by Kersti Frigell

Practice Book 92

A Division of The McGraw-Hill Companies

Columbus, Ohio

"Peep, peep, peep," calls the frog.
Ralph tells Phillip, "I found the phantom,
and it's a little green tree frog!"

8

181

Ralph looks closely at a leaf. "Hmm," he says. "I can take a photo of this frog."

183

In the spring, Phillip and Ralph take a hike in the woods.

3

The boys hear "Peep, peep, peep."
"I think it's a phantom," whispers Phillip.
"Don't be silly," scolds Ralph. "Phantoms are phony."

6

Phillip finds leaves like elephant ears.
Ralph takes photographs of birds in
the trees.

4

Then Phillip and Ralph hear "Peep,
peep, peep."
Ralph whispers, "It is not a bird."
Phillip asks Ralph, "What can it be?"

5

The Spider's Daughter

by Mike Wagner
illustrated by Shawn McManus

Practice Book 93

SRA

A Division of The McGraw-Hill Companies

Columbus, Ohio

Spider's daughter worked harder on her web.
Spider caught five flies. Her daughter caught six flies!

8

185

www.sra4kids.com

SRA/McGraw-Hill

A Division of The McGraw-Hill Companies

Copyright © 2002 by SRA/McGraw-Hill.

All rights reserved. Except as permitted under the United States Copyright Act, no part of this publication may be reproduced or distributed in any form or by any means, or stored in a database or retrieval system, without prior written permission from the publisher.

Printed in the United States of America.

Send all inquiries to:
SRA/McGraw-Hill
8787 Orion Place
Columbus, OH 43240-4027

Spider told her daughter, "Don't be naughty! We need good webs to catch our dinner."

Spider taught her daughter how to make a web from spider silk.

3

Spider taught her daughter how to make a new web.
Spider's daughter was naughty. She played with a beetle instead of working on her web.

6

4

Spider taught her daughter to make the silk threads firm and tight. Spider's daughter did not work hard on her web.

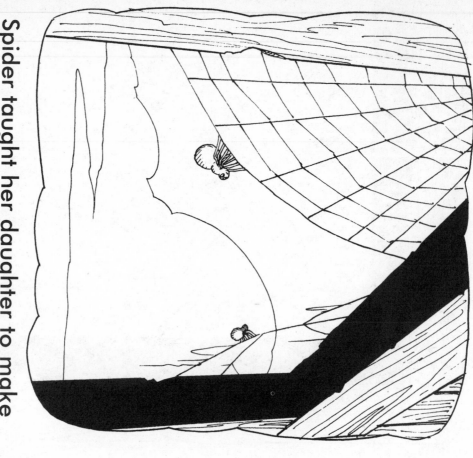

Spider caught five flies in her web. Spider's daughter did not catch a single fly.

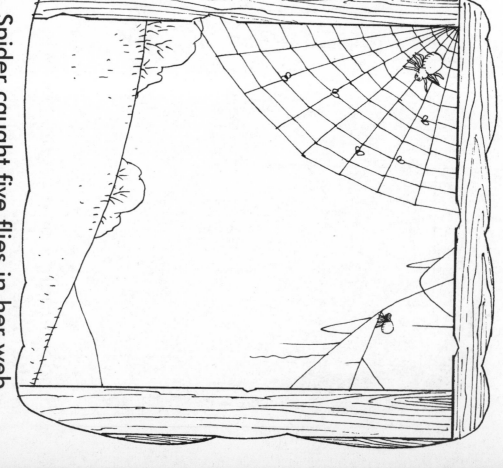

5

SRA Open Court Reading

Thoughtful Gifts

by Lucy Minor
illustrated by Olivia Cole

Practice Book 94

A Division of The McGraw-Hill Companies

Columbus, Ohio

189

Joe liked his terrific gifts.
He thanked his thoughtful pals.

8

www.sra4kids.com

SRA/McGraw-Hill

A Division of The McGraw-Hill Companies

Copyright © 2002 by SRA/McGraw-Hill.

Printed in the United States of America.

Send all inquiries to:
SRA/McGraw-Hill
8787 Orion Place
Columbus, OH 43240-4027

The children brought the gifts to Joe's birthday party. Joe's mom brought out the birthday cake.

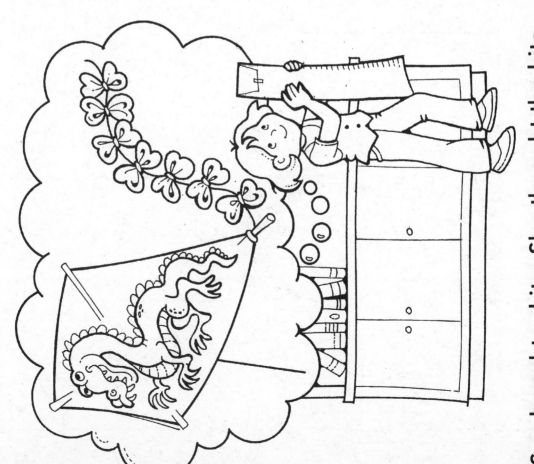

Kate, Mike, and Sue wanted to get
thoughtful gifts for Joe on his birthday.

3

Sue bought a kite. She thought the kite
looked like a dragon in the sky.

6

4

Kate bought a book about dinosaurs. The dinosaurs in the book fought a lot!

Mike bought a set of markers. He thought the markers looked like a rainbow.

5

SRA Open Court Reading

Pearl's Flowers

by Lucy Minor

illustrated by Pat Lucas-Morris

Practice Book 95

SRA

A Division of The McGraw-Hill Companies

Columbus, Ohio

Pearl learned to grow the best flowers on Earth!

8

193

www.sra4kids.com

SRA/McGraw-Hill

A Division of The McGraw-Hill Companies

Copyright © 2002 by SRA/McGraw-Hill.

All rights reserved. Except as permitted under the United States Copyright Act, no part of this publication may be reproduced or distributed in any form or by any means, or stored in a database or retrieval system, without prior written permission from the publisher.

Printed in the United States of America.

Send all inquiries to:
SRA/McGraw-Hill
8787 Orion Place
Columbus, OH 43240-4027

2

Pearl learned that earthworms help flowers grow.

7

SRA Open Court Reading

Pearl grew flowers in her garden.
She planted seeds in the earth.

3

Pearl saw earthworms.
She heard bees.

6

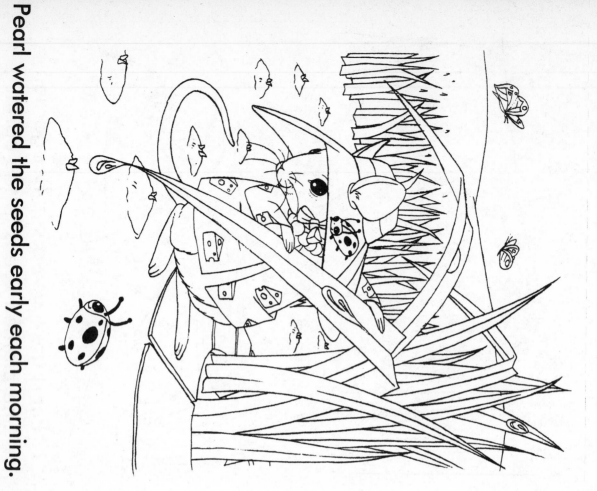

Pearl watered the seeds early each morning.

4

When the flowers grew, Pearl searched for weeds.

5

SRA Open Court Reading

Dudley the Donkey

by Rich Lewis
illustrated by Len Epstein

Practice Book 96

SRA

A Division of The McGraw-Hill Companies
Columbus, Ohio

"Dudley! Dudley! Are you going to help
me pull this cart of turkeys or not?"

8

2

The crowd will shout, "Dudley! Dudley!"
The crowd will throw me roses and carrots!

7

I'm Dudley the donkey.
I'm a jockey.

3

The winner will get fame and lots of cash.
Maybe the winner will even get a key to
the city.

6

4

Today I will race Abbey the turkey.
She is a jockey, too.

A big crowd has made the trip
to the valley to see the race.

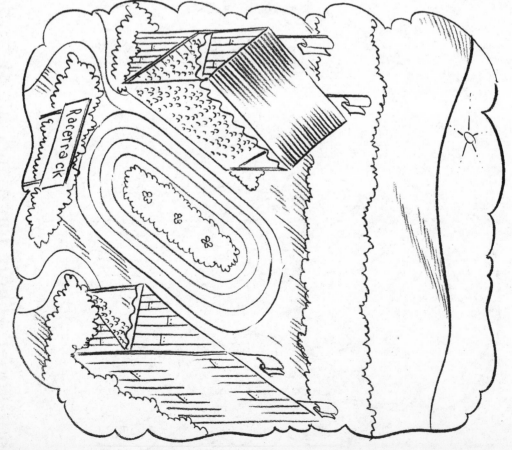

5

SRA Open Court Reading

The Skipper

by Harold Thomas
illustrated by Shawn McManus

Practice Book 97

A Division of The McGraw-Hill Companies

Columbus, Ohio

201

"Let's go, skipper. You and your companion here have had plenty of sailing this morning. It's time for lunch."

8

www.sra4kids.com

SRA/McGraw-Hill

A Division of The McGraw-Hill Companies

2

"Attention! I must mention that the action of the waves gives me motion sickness."

7

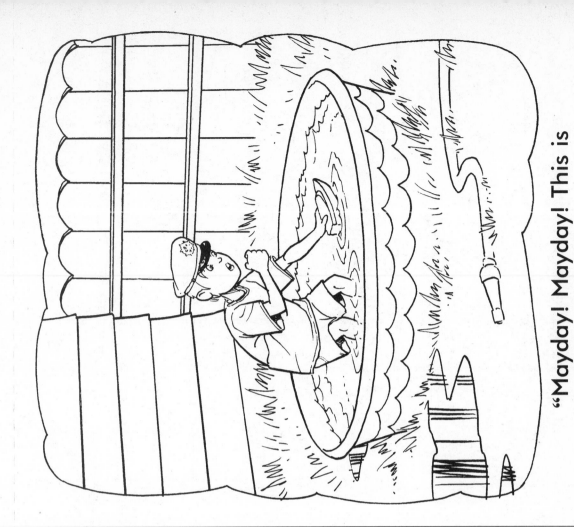

"Mayday! Mayday! This is 'Carter's Creation'."

3

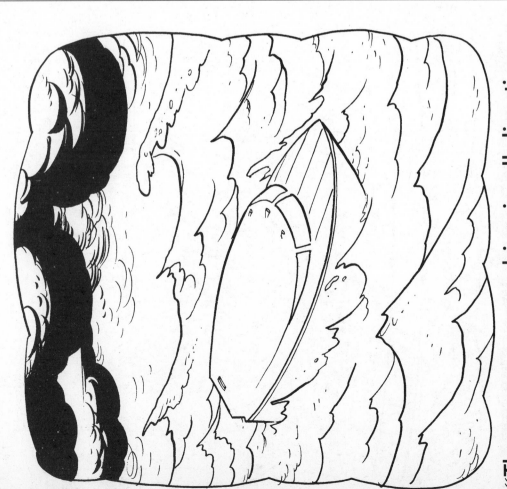

"The waves are crashing in all directions. I must use caution. The waves are at least three billion feet high!"

6

4

"Our position is five million miles away from land."

"The weather conditions are getting bad. In my opinion, we must get back to land quickly."

5